Zoom!

D0872894

FT Prentice Hall

FINANCIAL TIMES

In an increasingly competitive world, we believe it's quality of thinking that gives you the edge – an idea that opens new doors, a technique that solves a problem, or an insight that simply makes sense of it all. The more you know, the smarter and faster you can go.

That's why we work with the best minds in business and finance to bring cutting-edge thinking and best learning practice to a global market.

Under a range of leading imprints, including *Financial Times Prentice Hall*, we create world-class print publications and electronic products bringing our readers knowledge, skills and understanding, which can be applied whether studying or at work.

To find out more about Pearson Education publications, or tell us about the books you'd like to find, you can visit us at **www.pearson.com/uk**

PEARSON

Zoom!

THE FASTER WAY TO MAKE YOUR BUSINESS IDEA HAPPEN

Ian Sanders and David Sloly

Financial Times
Prentice Hall
is an imprint of

PEARSON

Harlow, England • London • New York • Boston • San Francisco • Toronto
Sydney • Tokyo • Singapore • Hong Kong • Seoul • Taipei • New Delhi
Cape Town • Madrid • Mexico City • Amsterdam • Munich • Paris • Milan

PEARSON EDUCATION LIMITED

EDINBURGH GATE

HARLOW CM20 2JE

TEL: +44 (0)1279 623623

FAX: +44 (0)1279 431059

WEBSITE: WWW.PEARSON.COM/UK

FIRST PUBLISHED IN GREAT BRITAIN IN 2011

© IAN SANDERS AND DAVID SLOLY 2011

THE RIGHTS OF IAN SANDERS AND DAVID SLOLY TO BE IDENTIFIED AS AUTHORS OF THIS WORK HAVE BEEN
ASSERTED BY THEM IN ACCORDANCE WITH THE COPYRIGHT, DESIGNS AND PATENTS ACT 1988.

PEARSON EDUCATION IS NOT RESPONSIBLE FOR THE CONTENT OF THIRD-PARTY INTERNET SITES.

ISBN: 978-0-273-75567-8

BRITISH LIBRARY CATALOGUING-IN-PUBLICATION DATA
A CATALOGUE RECORD FOR THIS BOOK IS AVAILABLE FROM THE BRITISH LIBRARY

LIBRARY OF CONGRESS CATALOGING-IN-PUBLICATION DATA
Sanders, Ian, 1968-
  Zoom : the faster way to make your business idea happen / Ian Sanders and David Sloly.
    p. cm.
  Includes index.
  ISBN 978-0-273-75567-8 (pbk.)
  1. New business enterprises. 2. Entrepreneurship. 3. Marketing. I. Sloly, David. II. Title.
  HD62.5.S27156 2011
  658.1'1--dc23
                          2011030726

ALL RIGHTS RESERVED. NO PART OF THIS PUBLICATION MAY BE REPRODUCED, STORED IN A RETRIEVAL
SYSTEM, OR TRANSMITTED IN ANY FORM OR BY ANY MEANS, ELECTRONIC, MECHANICAL,PHOTOCOPYING,
RECORDING OR OTHERWISE, WITHOUT EITHER THE PRIOR WRITTEN PERMISSION OF THE PUBLISHER
OR A LICENCE PERMITTING RESTRICTED COPYING IN THE UNITED KINGDOM ISSUED BY THE COPYRIGHT
LICENSING AGENCY LTD, SAFFRON HOUSE, 6–10 KIRBY STREET, LONDON EC1N 8TS. THIS BOOK MAY NOT BE
LENT, RESOLD, HIRED OUT OR OTHERWISE DISPOSED OF BY WAY OF TRADE IN ANY FORM OF BINDING OR
COVER OTHER THAN THAT IN WHICH IT IS PUBLISHED, WITHOUT THE PRIOR CONSENT OF THE PUBLISHER.

ALL TRADEMARKS USED HEREIN ARE THE PROPERTY OF THEIR RESPECTIVE OWNERS. THE USE OF ANY
TRADEMARK IN THIS TEXT DOES NOT VEST IN THE AUTHORS OR PUBLISHER ANY TRADEMARK OWNERSHIP
RIGHTS IN SUCH TRADEMARKS, NOR DOES THE USE OF SUCH TRADEMARKS IMPLY ANY AFFILIATION WITH
OR ENDORSEMENT OF THIS BOOK BY SUCH OWNERS.

10 9 8 7 6 5 4 3 2 1
15 14 13 12 11

ILLUSTRATIONS BY ZOË SANDERS
TYPESET IN 9.5pt SWISS 721 BT LIGHT BY 30

PRINTED BY ASHFORD COLOUR PRESS LTD, GOSPORT

Contents

Shout outs

Thanks for sharing your story: Elizabeth Varley, Jeffrey Kalmikoff, John Vincent, Richard Moross and Will King. Thanks to everyone else we spoke to who we featured in the book: Chris White, Dave Stewart, David Heinemeier Hansson, Fred Wilson, Gary Vaynerchuk, Guy Kawasaki, James Barlow, Kevin Roberts, Pascal Grierson, Preethi Nair, Sarah Beeny, Tom Peters and Tony Hsieh.

Thanks to SXSW for starting the whole thing off; to Liz Gooster for having faith in the idea; to Simon Trewin for advice. Thanks to Zoë Sanders for her doodles.

Ian would like to thank Zoë, Barney and Dylan for their love and general putting up with him; giving him the space to make this idea happen.

David would like to thank Annette and Hunter. Annette for asking lots of questions and Hunter for asking none at all.

Thanks to Paris, Austin, London, Bristol and Leigh-on-Sea and far too many espressos for inspiration.

The birth of Zoom!

So this is how it all started.

ZOOM SNAPSHOT #1

March 2010. The Hilton Hotel, Austin, Texas

We're in a green room at South by Southwest ('SXSW') in Austin, Texas – a festival known for making bands, films and ideas famous. David Sloly and Ian Sanders don't have a band or a film (yet); we're here to evangelise our belief that anyone looking to make their business idea happen, should 'unplan it', ditching traditional strategic planning for the best business strategy of all: just doing it. We're about to enter a conference room to start our 'How to Unplan Your Business' session: we're not sure what the audience is going to make of our crazy idea, but we're passionate about sharing it. And that's a damn good place to start.

ZOOM SNAPSHOT #2

September 2010. The Hospital Club, Covent Garden, London

SXSW went well, our accompanying ebook has been read by more than 5,000 people and got others talking; some like it, others loathe it. Today we're waiting to meet a publisher who may or may not turn this idea into a physical book. if you're reading this, and it says 'Financial Times Prentice Hall' on the spine that means she liked it :)

The journey to getting our idea out there has been a lesson in just getting it done, we didn't approach it with a complicated grand plan.

We had an idea and we made it happen:

→ We didn't wait for 'permission' to get started; we set up a blog and started capturing thoughts and ideas, interviewing entrepreneurs and business owners.

→ We spotted an opportunity to share the idea at SXSW, so we submitted a proposal and got accepted.

→ We then decided to write a short book to accompany our session in Texas. We co-wrote a 20-page booklet, published it online and got 250 copies printed.

So we didn't wait 12 months to get a publishing deal; we just got on with launching and testing our idea in the marketplace. Then we spoke to Liz Gooster our publisher, but even that was random; we just got an email from her after following her on Twitter. (And we only followed Liz on Twitter because we saw she was connected to Dave Stewart who Ian had just met. And Ian had only met Dave because he was stranded in London from the 'ash cloud'. And Ian had only contacted Dave because he saw him walking down Wardour Street in Soho that day, etc. You get the idea... it's a typically random tale.)

And that random tale is no different from thousands of similar ones: of how people make their own ideas happen. Our journey from first thought to this book has been a great metaphor and experiment for what we're calling 'Zoomology': taking an idea, shaping it and making it happen.

Why listen to us?

We're the *Zoom* guys and we have been involved
in many successful start-ups. Some businesses we
launched for ourselves and some we launched for
other people. We've helped companies refocus to
make them profitable in changing markets. We've
helped one man start-ups see a goal clearly and
take the right action to reach it. We've been involved
in boardroom battles, witnessed first hand hostile
takeovers and led award-winning successes. We've
generated ideas and made those ideas happen
for global brands and many much, much smaller
less famous companies. We have studied creativity,
strategy, business owners and psychotherapy in our
pursuit to make fast business launches a reality. Now

we want to share with you all our insights, real world experiences and truths, all aimed at getting your business launched faster.

THE AUTHORS ON THE AUTHORS

David on Ian

I first met Ian whilst working as a creative at a start-up media company. Ian asked far too many questions for my liking but he had a knack of being able to deduce profitable opportunities from his quick fire questions and then act on them quickly. I liked that, you see, with a surname like mine (Sloly pronounced 'slowly') you learn very early in life that procrastination of any kind only gives people the ammunition they need to say 'Sloly by name...' and that has a danger of sticking. So Ian, quizzing me constantly to one side, was the kind of guy that I could work with. Back then no one was that sure what he actually did all day but he soon carved out a niche for soaking up all those projects no one else knew what to do with. He likes to cross disciplines, taking new approaches to work and business; he's now in the 'light bulb' business where he comes up with ideas to boost clients' businesses.

He is fast, very business driven and intelligent. He also shares my passion for coffee.

www.iansanders.com

Ian on David

I first met David in 1993 at a media group where he was then freelancing. I soon discovered this was a guy with bucket loads of ideas, most of them good. In many ways David was ahead of his time; as a then staff producer he suggested to his boss he go and brainstorm some ideas for radio shows sitting by a lake. His boss said he had to stay at his desk. He left and went on to produce an award winning show for another company (who let him work by the lake). I admire his appetite for breaking the rules and to carve out a working life beyond broadcasting to embrace the advertising industry and more recently psychotherapy. Not many have that courage and the talent to pull it off. So when I was seeking a partner in crime for a new project; for someone to challenge and stimulate me in equal measures, it was Sloly I called. David is Executive Creative Director – 'Head of Big Ideas' basically – at the technology marketing agency, Mason Zimbler.

www.sloly.com

introduction

LAUNCHING A BUSINESS HAS JUST GOT QUICKER

Is launching your business feeling like a slow process? Does it feel like you may run out of time and money before the cash starts flowing? Are you wondering 'what's next' as you navigate the muddy waters of a business start-up? If you have answered yes to any of the above, then this book is for you. Zoom! The Faster Way to Make Your Business Idea Happen is packed with powerful tools and techniques that will help you get your business up and running quickly.

Jeffrey Kalmikoff – who we'll feature in more detail later on – said that the definition of 'business' is the mechanism for taking an idea from concept to reality. We like that.

So, welcome to *Zoom!*, the book that will show you how to quickly get your business up and running and making money. Whether your business idea is for a product or service, a hobby business, a small business, big business or a brand new idea, *Zoom!* will guide you to your goal of making your idea a reality in the quickest time possible. It cuts out the waste, addresses the common fears, warns you of typical mistakes made by others and demonstrates modern techniques that will lead you to achieve success quickly.

The world is full of people with ideas for a business. As you read this page, eureka moments are happening in showers, train carriages and coffee shops around the globe. But for many, the business idea that appeared like a lightning strike in the mind will stay just that – an idea in someone's mind. The very fact that you're reading a book called *Zoom! The Faster Way to Make Your Business Idea Happen* means you actually want to do something with your business idea. You want to make it real. And you don't want to follow the old rules of making your business happen. When we talk about 'business' we aren't talking about Wall Street, towering office blocks, PowerPoint presentations or 200-page business plans. We aren't talking about TV shows like *Dragons' Den* or *The Apprentice*, where people are reduced to begging for money or grovelling for acceptance. We are not talking about too many people sitting around a boardroom table taking an hour to reach a decision and then three months to implement it. We are talking about doing business *your* way, which in this newer flatter Internet world means the way that suits you. Speed and simplicity is our focus and we want it to be yours because procrastination of a business idea is the surest way to kill it dead. Once you get momentum – which by order of you reading this means you've already started – you will get to ride that wave all the way to launch and beyond. It will be fun, interesting and rewarding, but most of all, it will be fast.

Today's business start-up success stories are not born out of great knowledge or education, they're about having the right mindset and attitude. *Zoom!* will show you how to fine-tune your mindset so you can fast-track your journey to make your new business happen. All the tools and techniques are right here.

Everything in this book has been written to help you reach your goal of launching your business as quickly as possible. We understand that time really is money, your money. So we will show you how to achieve your goal as quickly and effectively as possible.

To create this guide we've interviewed small business owners, big business owners, serial entrepreneurs and venture capitalists; in fact every kind of person who has launched a business, big or small. We have studied business owners who have launched post recession to understand how they navigated through these difficult times to achieve success. We have looked at the latest free business tools that will speed up the journey and cut down on your spending. We have studied the way modern entrepreneurs work and here we're going to share what we've learnt.

We've learnt that agility beats the big guys at their own game and in this book we show you how to think and act agile. We learnt that the human mind is so risk adverse that it fears success as much as failure. To combat this human condition we will share with you powerful techniques that will give you the mindset to make your business goals real. We learnt that those who make decisions quickly get more of the right stuff done and we have included easy ways to enable you to make better and faster decisions.

We'll explain how you can take your passion, hobby or idea and make money by turning it into a business and we will only talk about techniques that make your business start-up journey smarter and faster. So those long-winded old-fashioned ways of starting a business, those styles that originated from the industrial revolution, they're not in this book.

So stop thinking how many years it will take to launch your business, or even how many months it will take, fasten your seat belts and get ready to launch your business in just 60 days.

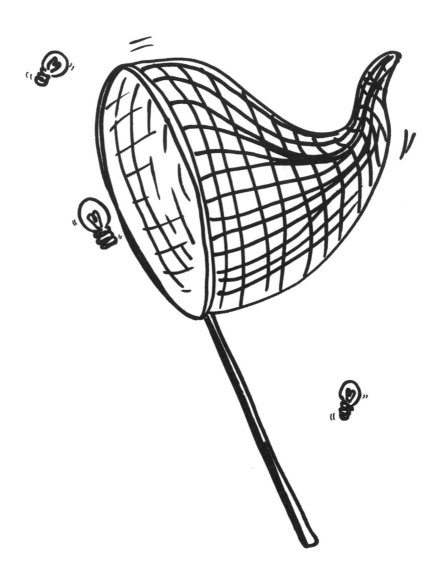

Creating your eureka moment

HOW TO CATCH AN IDEA

It all starts with an idea, right? You woke up one morning with an idea that could make you money and now you want to make it real. Or maybe you were sitting at work and – 'bingo' – an idea came to you in a flash and before you leave your job you want to read how you can quickly make that bingo moment real.

So many reasons, so many ideas, so many opportunities to launch a business, a business that will have an impact. Your business is going to change lives (starting with your own). It may be in a small way, like provide enough passive income to pay for a better holiday next year or it may change it in a huge way, like beating the big guys with a game-changing alternative to a mass-market product. That's the potential of where your business can take you. But the exciting bit is where it starts and it all starts with an idea.

But just because it started small, never underestimate its power and potential. Whatever popular culture may have told you, ideas are not exclusive to the creatives, the arts or the ultra hip. They are everywhere and for the collection by anyone. We hear many people say that they can never have good ideas. That's a myth, something you may have been told by a teacher who mistook ideas for mastering formulas, it may be something a parent said in an effort to stop you doing something risky or it may be a partner, frustrated at their own lack of seizing the moment. The reality is we all have ideas; we are programmed by nature to solve problems, and to solve problems you need an idea. So OK, you may be a bit rusty, but you still have ideas.

All ideas start the same way. Let's look at the idea behind Coca-Cola. Sure, it's world famous now, but it started small. Legend has it that pharmacist Dr John Pemberton was in his home laboratory trying to make a remedy for headaches. He ended up with a caramel syrup that when mixed with carbonated water tasted quite nice. Dr Pemberton went on to sell his drink in the local soda store and it wasn't until the potential of his recipe was picked up by someone else that it started the journey to world fame. It certainly wasn't an obvious recipe for success yet last year there were 1.6 billion servings of Coca-Cola sold every day. All that from an idea! Just as Coca-Cola started life as nothing more than an idea, so Harry Potter started life as an idea in J.K. Rowling's mind, the Internet started as an idea in the mind of Sir Timothy Berners-Lee, in fact, everything man-made you have seen since you woke up this morning, everything large and small started as an idea in someone's mind.

Think about it.

The idea you have does not need to be groundbreaking. It could be a better way of doing something or it could be taking an existing product or service to a new audience. For example, you don't need to invent a new drink, you may just note that there isn't a coffee shop near you; with lots of people locally who want to buy one, you set a coffee shop up. Not every business needs to be a new idea.

not every business needs to be a new idea

So now you have an idea; the next thing a *Zoom!* reader needs to learn is the importance of doing something about an idea.

If an idea stays an idea in your mind, and you do nothing about it then it is powerless. It won't change lives locked in there. You need to make it happen. And that's what this book is all about.

Your idea might be ridiculed or rejected by people you share it with. That's not a bad thing. When we were championing our idea that businesses should forget business planning, we got a message on Twitter saying our idea was 'dangerous rubbish'. We knew then that we were on to something. People will always try and arrest your idea, for so many reasons. Family and friends may be afraid that should your idea be successful you will change, and they don't want you to change. Or they may be afraid your idea will fail, and they don't want to see you fail. Wonderful. So instead they encourage you to do nothing.

So once you start evangelising about your idea, be prepared for some negativity. You know the kind of thing. 'Do you think that's sensible, to quit your job in this climate?' or 'I was reading in the newspaper that 90% of new businesses fail in the first year' or 'A musical dog bowl – are you sure that's going to make you a millionaire?'. So you're going to need thick skin to deal with all this. You'll also need a support network – people who will not knock your idea down with doom-mongering statistics, but people who will share your optimism and make your idea even better. Later in the book we will point you in the direction of this important group – they are fellow Zoomers, real people who one person at a time are changing the fortunes of our nation. They will have ideas that are life-changing, new and interesting or just outright strange. But that's OK, the world needs and will pay for them all. So embrace Zoom, not doom! Don't kill your idea just because it may not meet the social norms.

> zoomers, real people who one person at a time are changing the fortunes of our nation

Can you imagine the reaction the inventor of the Magic Tree received when he first told family and friends that he had an idea to manufacture a five inch scented tree that will hang from the rear view mirror of a car? They probably thought he was losing the plot and would have actively encouraged him not to give up the day job. Yet, according to legend, when a milk truck driver who had had enough of the smell of spilt milk mentioned it to a local chemist Julius Sämann, he invented the scented tree that now hangs in cars all over the world. How many people slapped their foreheads and said 'Doh, why didn't I think of that?' So yes, people may laugh but now that inventor sits in his pine scented mansion paid for by Magic Trees.

Sometimes it may take your idea to mix with someone else's experience to make it real. So don't be afraid to talk to people about your idea, share it as you hone it.

Just as the Magic Tree relied on two people to make it happen, many other business ideas were the result of two people's thoughts and experiences colliding. The 'Post-it' Note was developed by Spencer Silver and

Art Fry at 3M; Spencer developed the science for the peel and stick ability; Art delivered 'the application' that made it a popular paper product around the office. It needed both contributions to be game-changing; by itself the peel and stick molecular structure was not a product that could be commoditised. Art Fry had used the adhesive to make a stickable bookmark. That was OK but it wasn't until he used the bookmark to write a question and stick it to the front of a report and his supervisor responded on the same sticky note, that the real eureka moment arrived. So don't lock your idea in a filing cabinet or a password-protected document: let it run wild and bump into people.

Other innovations come about from that classic entrepreneurial trait, coming up with answers to problems. Will King, the guy behind the 'King of Shaves' brand created a business to fix a problem. Fed up with suffering razor burn from regular shaving products he experimented with his girlfriend's bath oil and devised a shaving oil. He didn't know anything about the shaving business, but he knew he'd buy his own product, and he reckoned there were other men like him. The naysayers didn't believe he could compete with the market leaders like Gillette but that didn't deter him. In fact, it spurred Will on to turn his dream into reality, and as we write this we just saw on Twitter he's on a flight to the States to take his brand global.

So let's get your ideas working for you right now. First you need to get on the right wavelength to recognise ideas, to catch them in your butterfly net, because they won't always be that obvious. Not all successful ideas are jaw-dropping, they won't have a spotlight illuminating them on a stage or a neon arrow over them. More likely it'll be a gentle thought that arrives, grows and develops until that light bulb flashes bright and you realise what you have got. So be ready to catch those ideas. Are you a notepad or iPad kind of

you need to get on the right wavelength to recognise ideas

person, do you need a bunch of people in a room with a marker pen and flip chart or do you need to sit in a library with books? What is it going to take?

For musician and creative entrepreneur Dave Stewart, his method isn't that obvious. He told us,

> *The way that I think is kind of conceptual at the beginning. I don't think, 'Oh, I've got a great idea for a business.' Instead, I'll draw a picture of something. And then I'll give it a title. And then it'll slowly become something. It might turn into a song, it might turn into an idea for a movie, it might turn into a hundred different things. But I keep adding to it, and the picture becomes clearer. So I'm working back to front.*

Whilst history may have brought technological innovation, the principles behind ideas have stayed the same. Over 40 years ago James Webb Young wrote in his book, *A Technique for Producing Ideas*, that an idea is nothing more, nor less, than a new combination of old elements. According to him the process has five stages:

1   Gather as much raw information as possible: this involves being a detective and finding out lots of stuff about the problem or opportunity. Not just time on a search engine, but asking people how the problem effects them.

2   Chew it over and get your first ideas out of your system: once you understand the problem, some solutions may just appear real fast. These may not be the real answer you are capable of delivering. They may be just your first thoughts. Write them down, but proceed to the next stage before acting upon them.

3   Stop thinking about the subject and let your subconscious go to work: this is the easy bit. Just forget about the whole thing. Your subconscious will now go to work looking for a solution to the problem.

4   Be ready for ideas to flow at any time: carry a pen and paper. Even have one handy in the shower (you can find waterproof pens and pads at many sites or stores selling accessories for divers).

5   Shape and develop the idea for practical usefulness: take your raw idea and share it with others to help shape it and make it fit for purpose.

If you want to turn your idea into a business, that 'practical usefulness' is essential. It's no use having a great idea that serves no purpose.

But whatever path you take to devising your genius idea, it has to get you excited. Will it get you up at 6 a.m. in the morning in the middle of winter? Will it have you reaching for your notepad in the middle of the night? Does it give you 'goose bumps'? And if not, maybe it's not good enough.

ZOOM THINKING

1   Have you addressed the problem your product or business is trying to solve?

2   Why will your customers love it?

3   Are you in love with the idea?

ZOOM IN ON... WILL KING

'Rocking the boulder'

Twitter: @kingofshaves

Web: shave.com

Lots of people dream about creating a product that will sit on the supermarket shelves alongside established brands; not many people pull it off. Will King set up his shaving-oils business, King of Shaves, 18 years ago after being made redundant. Suffering from razor burn and experimenting with his girlfriend's bath oil, he developed a shaving oil. But success did not come overnight: in his first year he sold just 150 bottles and lost £30,000, and he continued to lose money for those first five years. But he's come a long way: his brand achieved sales of £13m in the 17 months to May 2010, he has 10% of the UK market and is now expanding into the US.

Will told us that success involves a long-term strategy and luck; after those difficult first five years, he manged to 'rock the boulder out of the hollow'. Once it rocked, it gained momentum, and rocked again. He kept on rocking it, the business became profitable, then profit doubled the next year, and again.

Will's tips for faster, easier ways to make you business idea happen:

1 Don't focus on making money; focus on making a great product. Money is the by-product of a great product.

2 Have a motivator. For Will it's a desire to shape his own destiny together with his dream of designing the BatYacht, a Batman-concept super yacht.

3 Exploit 'smarketing'. Harness social media to have a dialogue with your audience online.

4 Embrace your single-minded proposition. For the King of Shaves, that means the brand is about your best shave; that informs everything from product innovation to quality.

Video interview with Will at **thezoomguys.com**.

The trouble with too much planning

HOW TO UNPLAN YOUR BUSINESS

Danger: you are about to start developing and writing a business plan. STOP. A lesson we have learnt is that doing is much more powerful than planning. We are going to show you why action is much more beneficial to you right now than a detailed business plan.

If over-planning is a business killer what is the new business *giver*?

Two years ago a leaflet dropped through David's front door just as he was about to sit down to breakfast. It contained a comprehensive list of evening classes available in his local area: photography for beginners, flower arranging, pottery, you get the idea. On that list he noticed a course entitled 'How to plan a business'. The year was 2009 and the economic world was moving at lightning speed and in the wrong direction. David scribbled the letters 'UN' in front of the word plan so that it read, 'How to UNplan a business', finished his breakfast and left for work. That evening over dinner his wife Annette, who too had looked through the leaflet, asked why he had changed 'plan' to 'unplan'? What's the point of a business plan David asked? If you had a three-year business plan that you wrote nine months ago where exactly in it did you write 'the world economy collapses'? Do you create a column to add 'banks stop lending' or 'shareholders panic'?. No; the notion of these long-term plans in a fast moving world just seemed plain broken. What people need is a goal, not a plan. That little idea, that single thought could have easily died a death there and then. But David felt passionate about it and later that week started talking with Ian. It resonated with Ian because he'd never had a plan for his career or business. Ian joined in the debate and together they got quite animated about this ridiculous thought that people think they can predict the future just because they have spent excessive time writing a detailed business plan. The business plan for Hotmail was written overnight by one of the founders, Sabeer Bhatia. It was enough to secure finances to hire programmers to create the webmail service that was later sold for $400 million to Microsoft. The world is full of businesses that began without a plan. They had a goal, a desire, a passion, but no business plan.

the notion of these long-term plans in a fast moving world just seemed plain broken

Six months later, we were invited to Austin, Texas to give a talk at South by Southwest, an annual music, film, and interactive conference and festival. Yes, that little scribble David had made, the animated conversation with Ian that followed, it had now turned into something real. Now it was a presentation that would be scrutinised by some of the smartest entrepreneurs in the world. We opened our talk by asking for a show of hands relating to business owners and their business plans. More than 60% of entrepreneurs attending our session didn't have a business plan and the 40% that did admitted never looking at it after writing it. Successful, intelligent business owners, gathered in a room, happy to come clean that the business plan wasn't worth the paper it was written on; in agreement that their time would have been better spent by business doing rather than business planning. How on earth can you plan three or five years in the future in such a rapidly changing world? We talked to Gary Vaynerchuk who runs a hugely successful wine business Wine Library and a consulting business VaynerMedia alongside a web TV show, a radio show and he is also a business book author. Gary told Ian in the back of the car heading from Heathrow:

A Five Year Plan is impossible in a world where what five years represents is so different than it used to. We're going through a technology explosion, and you can't possibly do that; think about what five years ago looked like.

Gary explained that instead he stays open minded to opportunities, always ready to embrace change: his core strength is being a 'reactionary businessman'. Being reactionary is about being ready for action, ready to react to situations to take advantage of opportunities that land in your lap. It's having the right attitude to spot an opportunity and go for it; to adapt to economic, technological and market changes. With a rigid fixed plan mindset, that's difficult. Keeping flexible and open minded is the way to succeed. Or you will risk missing out on business opportunities. We cover this in the detail it deserves in Chapter 8 'Think like a speedboat'.

So why do we plan? Simply put, we plan to attempt to eliminate uncertainty: the things you can't predict or guarantee. Some think that by creating a plan for executing your business idea you will somehow guarantee its success, or at least spot the potential problems. But let's be honest. We also plan because we're told that's what entrepreneurs, department heads and CEOs do. We need plans to show investors, our bosses and the Board. Plans make us appear accountable. But in a fast-moving world, such plans are fast becoming meaningless. A friend of ours, Pascal Grierson, recently launched French Radio London, a French-speaking radio station in London. Over a beer in a Parisian café we asked him what business plan he had. Pascal shrugged his shoulders the way only a Frenchman can and informed us that he had one side of paper with two sections. One was 'the why' and the other, 'the who': why London needed a French radio station; and who will make it happen. As soon as he told us that London is the sixth biggest French-speaking city in the world, we realised that was a compelling reason to open a French-speaking radio station in London. The 'who' was Pascal, with 20 years' experience in broadcasting. With that clarity of mindset, he got his investors and London got a French-speaking radio station.

In contrast to Pascal, a friend (who shall remain nameless) was attempting to launch a business. He had a great new idea that was potentially game changing for that particular industry and offered huge commercial potential. But he's been very busy planning, thinking of every eventuality, and it still isn't launched! Every time we see him, he has a new reason he hasn't launched: the site is being re-tested, the navigation has changed, he got tired of the logo. It drives us mad: why doesn't he just launch the bloody thing? He needs to refocus on why that original idea he had in the pub two years ago was so compelling. But too much time and too much analysis have slowed things down. Analysis can be paralysing: over thinking an idea will lead to self-doubt.

> analysis can be paralysing: over thinking an idea will lead to self-doubt

Guy Kawasaki is the former chief evangelist of Apple who is now a venture capitalist at Garage Technology Ventures in Silicon Valley where he invests in some of the most cutting-edge technology companies in the world. Guy told us his frustrations seeing entreprenuers pitch their business plans:

Many entrepreneurs show up to us with these 'magna carta' size business plans; they've spent two weeks cranking out a spreadsheet so they have this Excel sheet that says five years out, times 12 months, times 200 line items... they're going to tell you how much to spend on pencils in the fourth month of the fifth year! And you know what, basically, I know they're making it up.

The human mind is fantastic at taking a problem, seeing a pattern and figuring out a solution. Keep pushing more and more information at the same problem and it quickly gets to the point where your brain – more complex, faster and more powerful then any computer invented by any person – can't make an educated guess anymore. It just analyses more and more information, stifling any hope of using its real function of being able to take an educated guess. An educated guess based on all you have learnt through life, all the wisdom you have soaked up along that fascinating journey. Don't become the victim of over analysing and reaching the analysis paralysis deadlock: people who think they must have every scrap of information before they can make a decision, people who believe they must weigh every possible piece of information against every possible outcome. Those people, and we all know one, tend to tell you about great ideas they have had yet done nothing about. They have failed to realise any of those ideas because they have over analysed them to the point that they are stuck in a knowledge trap.

the people that succeed recognise they don't have all the answers and probably never will, but pursue anyway

The people that succeed, the ones that don't get stuck at first base are the ones that recognise they don't have all the answers and probably never will, but pursue anyway. And the tool those people use? – Instinct. Believe us when we say instinct is an incredibly useful tool to have in your toolkit.

37signals is a software company based in Chicago that has become legendary by creating productivity tools and books that are used by companies around the world. They launched in 1999 as a web design business but soon pivoted to sell the productivity tools they'd initially developed for in-house use. 37signals has achieved success by reinventing their offering and keeping their operation lean. We asked partner David Heinemeier Hansson, what role instinct has played in their success.

> *We rely heavily on instinct. An instinct that has been developed and formed from a decade in business. Sometimes careful analysis is helpful, but often times you're just trying to justify what your instinct is already telling you. Why not follow that straight from the get go?*

An idea that never gets launched because you can't make your mind up if you should have a red website background or a blue one; if the logo should be a bird or a butterfly; if the business card should be gloss or matt, is worthless. Yep, you heard us right – it's worth nothing. Nothing more than a distraction. All it will ever be is an idea gathering dust: you have to **do something** with it. If you're not risking too much money or staking your family home or reputation on it, what's to lose? Isn't it worth getting your idea out there?

Success isn't about how good your business plan is on paper, it's about having the courage to make the leap. It's the ones doing something about their idea that are succeeding; the ones that didn't bother? They didn't stand a chance.

ZOOM THINKING

1　Promise yourself you will not spend time trying to guess the future.

2　Thinking back to Pascal's story, what is the 'Why' for your business?

3　What is the 'How' for your business?

Getting to grips with your mission

WHY YOU NEED TO UNDERSTAND WHAT'S DRIVING YOU

People are successful at launching and running businesses for one reason: they are driven. Without that drive, nothing will happen. The driving force that demands success and perseveres until you reach it is mainly emotional. It may be 15% rational, but it is 85% emotional. So does your idea get your heart racing?

A racing heart means you will be emotionally driven by the idea and emotion is a powerful motivator. If it doesn't turn you on, you won't make it a success, so you need to get tuned in to what flicks your entrepreneurial switch.

Napoleon Hill, the author of *Think and Grow Rich*, wrote:

People are influenced in their actions, not by reason so much as by feelings. The creative faculty of the mind is set into action entirely by emotions, and not by cold reason.

You need to remember that. The problem is that we don't tend to be very well trained in either harnessing the power of our emotions or listening to them with conviction. So you need to ask yourself some questions to identify your motives for why you are setting up a business. Your answers will help you understand your intentions and ensure you have the right motives and therefore motivation to be successful. Too many people jump in feet first without qualifying the Why and How they will succeed. This probably explains why so many start-ups fold in the first year and why so many manifestos for change in organisations start and end as a Word document with perhaps a scant attempt for implementation.

So why do you want to make your idea happen? There are many motivators you could choose from, for example:

Talent: some people have a talent or a skill and rather than supply that to another business to sell to a customer, they want to create a business for themselves.

Opportunity: they have spotted a niche in the market, an opportunity to create a game-changing product or provide a much need service.

understand your intentions and ensure you have the right motives and therefore motivation to be successful

Survival: Jay-Z talks about the values of a 'hustler', someone who does whatever it takes to succeed, investing the hours and hard grafting. Whether a street trader or a drug dealer (OK that may not be politically correct, but it's still a business) they're united by their ability and willingness to hustle.

Enterprise: maybe you just get a kick out of turning your thoughts into cash, of transforming an idea into an invoice? Perhaps you are driven by seeing those pound or dollar signs, that spreadsheet fill up with orders and revenues. You don't care what it takes, you just want to see the money fall into your account.

Passion: many people are so passionate about wine, or coffee, bicycles or skate boarding, they turn that into a business. They're driven by spending 18 hours a day engrossed in something they are so passionate about. They just love it.

Self-belief: we spoke to one entrepreneur who'd launched her business not out of a passion for a product but to prove her independence, to show everyone she could 'do it'. Like climbing Everest or running a marathon, they get rewarded by 'doing it'.

Collaboration: the buzz that comes from collaborating with others, being part of something bigger than themselves.

Philanthropic: you might have a yearning desire to help people or change the world; this can be a very powerful driver.

Creation: some are driven by the desire to create something, to see their idea come to fruition. The driver for us writing this book is the thought of seeing the finished product on the shelf, that helps motivate us when we suffer from writer's block.

Control: being in control of your own destiny – the notion that you can create the life you want to lead, doing your own thing.

So which one are you?

You looked at the list and worked out what's driving you – or what will drive you. But you also need to check out whether you are in the right place mentally and emotionally to take your idea forward.

Perhaps you've had this idea ticking away inside you for a long time – too long maybe – and you now know, it's time to commit, it's time to actually DO something about it. To make it happen, you need to have the right mindset.

You might be passionate about a business idea but haven't thought about what it might take to deliver it. Zoomology can help you speed along your journey of launching a new idea. But what happens once you are up and running? How much time will you need to keep things moving forward? Most new projects and start-ups suffer from total underestimation of the continued effort required to maintain and build success. So this area requires consideration now, before you go too far.

One of the biggest reasons we hear for people not pursuing their passion is that they don't have time. But we are all blessed with exactly the same amount of time in a day; it's just how we use it that differs. You need to figure out what must stay in your current routine and what can either go, like watching TV, or be carried out by another person. For example, could a cleaner save you three hours a week and that time be turned over to running the business?

Try keeping an honest diary during an average week. A diary that notes how you actually spend your waking hours. Start Monday morning and take brief notes in half hour blocks and then read through the results the following Monday. Now you can see clearly where your time is spent and what can be changed to accommodate your new workload.

Another consideration is your health. This journey isn't going to be easy – are you in the right place physically and mentally to launch a business? The stress associated with business in some instances can be high. It's not a question of are you able to cope, that's not good enough, it's are you able to thrive? If you are already suffering undue stress or anxiety then these issues must be addressed first. If necessary, seek help in lowering your stress levels to be better placed to ensure long-term success in your new venture.

For many a dream business is completely unrelated to what they have spent their entire working life doing. Simply put, they lack the right experience for their new venture. But don't be deterred: this doesn't need to interrupt your dream or dampen your passion. It's like David's story. David always wanted to be a hypnotherapist but worked in marketing. He was passionate about helping people get more from life and saw psychotherapy and hypnotherapy as a way of achieving that. He didn't want to give up his day job and go full-time as a hypnotherapist, but was willing to give up one evening a week to see clients. The set back was that he had none of the skills required; so he did some research until he found the right tutor. He took the course at the same time as remodelling his family home, getting married and accepting a promotion at work that would demand he learnt new skills. What drove him? Passion. A burning need that moved him forward each day, each week and over the course of the year until each task was complete. He qualified and began to see one client a week and that helping others provided him with great satisfaction. His wife testifies to this day that all during those times of learning, working on the house and changing job role he never complained once. He would rise at 6 a.m., go to the gym to clear his head and visualise his day ahead. Then he would work through the day, come home and work on the house until 9 p.m. From 9 until 10:30 p.m. he would study and go to bed. Sunday was a day for husband and wife. For one year: *no* TV, *no* unnecessary distractions, *no* excuses. That's not a boast: it's just proof that you CAN do it, if you have the right driver.

So if a knowledge vacuum is standing between you and your dreams, don't be put off. When you are enthusiastic and want to learn a subject you will be surprised just how quickly you can do it.

Funding is another hurdle that can come between you and what you want to do. You will need to work out the finances carefully: how much do you have, how long will it last and when do you expect to show a return on your investment. But this is not the book to educate you about business funding, there's an abundance of books that will go into granular detail on finances or you can talk to your friendly local accountants.

Apart from financial support, you'll need emotional and moral support. So surround yourself with others on a similar journey. When you do that, the conversation will become charged with energy and good ideas will flow. The support that loved ones and friends can give, although useful, cannot be matched by spending time with those on the same or similar path. This kind of networking is not about trying to persuade people to buy your product or service; it's about exchanging ideas and soaking up positive energy. You'll find people like this in your local coffee shop, co-working space or via online communities.

Does your idea fit with your personality – is it YOU? Does your personality complement your goals? For Sarah Beeny, launching a dating website mysinglefriend.com was just an extension of her personality. She told us she'd always set people up with friends and it seemed like fun to try and make a business off the back of that. When she ran out of single friends to introduce people to, she decided to set up a website to 'make life easier' for her network of friends. She repeated that philosophy with the launch of Tepilo.com, a property buying and selling website, when she was frustrated that people had to go through the costly process of using estate agents. Her idea bypassed that. She explained her approach for both businesses was simple:

> *I said: That's annoying [a website like that doesn't exist]. I'll build it.' But they're all things that interest me, they're not completely random.*

Her mantra about making things simple and easy to understand sits across all her business interests.

A friend of Ian's heard about a guy who was making lots of money from reselling goods online. The guy was buying goods from China, selling them through a website and shipping them to customers in Europe. He didn't even touch the goods. Ian's friend thought replicating this model would be cool. The problem? This is a very inhuman, commercially driven enterprise. You need to be excited just by £££ or $$$ and little else. It wasn't for his friend, it didn't excite him. So, ultimately, he didn't move forward with it. It hit the wall. It wasn't a good fit.

You need to constantly acknowledge the emotional trigger for your business: that's what will drive you forward. Because when things get tough, when you need to get up at 5:30 a.m. on a wet Monday morning to see a supplier, when you're working all weekend when you'd rather be spending time with the children: these are the moments that are going to make a difference to whether you fall flat on your face or sprint over the next hurdles. Recognising the emotional trigger will be the fuel for your tank that will keep you moving forward.

acknowledge the emotional trigger for your business: that's what will drive you forward

---

ZOOM THINKING

1 Promise yourself you will not get involved in a business that is not a natural fit.

2 Are you in the right mindset to start your business?

3 What are you prepared to sacrifice to succeed?

Set a goal

KNOWING WHERE YOU WANT TO GO IS THE FIRST STEP TO GETTING THERE

By now you've probably worked out that neither of us is a fan of detailed business plans. They tend to take too long to write and prove to be totally wrong when executed. So you might not need a plan, BUT you do need a goal. A goal gives you focus, something to fix on early in the game.

A goal gives you a destination, something to visualise on your journey. So identifying and articulating a goal at the very start is essential to your success. After all, if you don't know where you're going, how the heck are you going to get there?

In the epilogue of John Irving's novel, *Last Night in Twisted River*, Irving explains that he had the idea for the book in his head for 20 years. Twenty years! He'd written other novels in that period but he couldn't start writing this one until he had composed the last sentence. He didn't just need to know the end, he needed to know those final words. That's what it takes for John, he has to know the ending before he can begin the writing process. That way he knows where his story must go, its final destination. He calls this reverse road mapping. This echoes the advice of Kevin Roberts, CEO Worldwide at Saatchi & Saatchi with a great track record in launching new products and brands; Kevin told us, 'Start with the answer and work back.'

And whether a novel, a product, a shop, or a website, you need to do the same. Reverse road mapping: start at the end and work back. Every business client that we work with is subjected to a similar line of questioning. The questions we focus on asking help both parties gain a clear understanding of what the goal is. We want to know what a successful outcome looks like so that everyone knows when it's been achieved. Although our clients may give the goal a different name, such as Key Performance Indicators (KPIs), deadlines or metrics, what everyone wants to know is what success looks like. So what does success look like to you? Is it your first sale, a first booking, first invoice, first order, first customer?

Jeffrey Kalmikoff is an entrepreneur who helped build the T-shirt business Threadless, and now advises start-ups in the US. Jeffrey makes the point

he knows where his story must go, its final destination

that goals have to be realistic; about the difference between idealistic and realistic goals. Jeffrey told us: 'Setting goals is essential but the trick is about setting realistic achievable goals that outline a road map that gets you from point A to point B.' Jeffrey thinks you should be honest about what is achievable – 'For example, "reaching 1 million users" is an idealistic goal when you have 1 thousand users. Setting goals that represent shorter steps and ultimately a series of small successes is a great way to keep motivation and momentum high.'

That goal setting fits in with our salami-slicing approach in Chapter 10, celebrating milestones along the way. Our goal was to write this book but our publisher made it easier for us by saying every three weeks we need to submit five chapters. That's more achievable than 20 chapters in a single go, right? We've got those dates down on our diary, it's good, and it gives us a clear view of what we need to do. It gives us focus so that we don't find ourselves distracted and then panic when the delivery date suddenly creeps up on us. It creates just the right amount of pressure required to sleep well at night and still deliver in the morning. So as early as possible you will want to get a view of what the end of your project, or the next part of your project, looks like, the outcome, success. Then you can map a way to get there.

get a view of what the end of your project, or the next part of your project, looks like

Making your goal tangible will help you appreciate it when you achieve it: 'I'm going to open my shop'; 'we're going to launch our website'; 'I'm going to have a paying customer'; 'my product will be available through Amazon'. They are clear, finite and there's no ambiguity. Your product available to buy through Amazon is the goal. If your product is sitting in a container in the Atlantic or stuck in a warehouse in Manchester, you haven't met your goal. If your goal lacks clarity or purpose, it won't be an enabler for you to reach your destination. Unclear goals lead people to adopt a 'plan B' opt out. Plan B opt outs sounds like this, 'if my business idea doesn't "work out" I can always go back to my old career, last job, benefits'. But the goal is not clear. What does 'work out' really mean? When you have no clear goals set your thoughts will end up focusing in on the plan B. When you let your mind focus on the plan B you will be guided to that goal. Military generals know that if you want the greatest chance of success on the battlefield, it is best not to have a plan B. Generals talk of sailing to the shore of the battle and then burning the ships on arrival so that the troops know that there is no turning back. No plan B. Win or die becomes the battle cry rather than have a go and jump back on the ship if the going gets tough.

Knowing what you want your outcome to be gives you plain vision of your goal. But more than that, it will let you see if you are on track to reaching it or if you are going off track. In which case you can adjust your course to be better aligned to reach your goal. That vision of your goal is important, it is an enabler that will give you confidence and assurance that what you are doing is right and you can continue or what you are doing is wrong and you must make a change. A focused ethic keeps you on a clear path to your goal, once your goal is achieved you are free to move on to the next one. This focused approach is a good strategy: we've heard it referred to as 'Nail it then scale it', and we like that. Focus on a single goal, once you've reached it – and only then – can you focus on growing it, scaling it. This is the fast way to success. The slow way is to have vague goals and meander around without direction.

So what is your goal?

Now you have your goal, or list of goals, you need to put them in to context by applying a time frame. If your goal is to sell personalised wax candles online and you have no time frame in which to execute this business idea, then it will take you as long as it takes to launch. Which may turn out to be three weeks, or equally it may turn out to be three years. The goal gives our minds the focus. Couple the goal together with a time line and we think you will agree that the two become a powerful driver for giving you the very best chance of achieving what you want from your business in the fastest time. Real goals leave no ambiguity, they require sweat and commitment to complete. But once you've set it, there's no other choice than to hit it. No alternative. You've just got to lean into the task and do it.

real goals leave no ambiguity, they require sweat and commitment to complete

So how long should you allow for your new business start-up? What kind of time frame should you be working in? For most modern businesses, using the Internet, supplying a service or product that does not require inventing, manufacturing and proving we believe that 60 days is enough.

If that sounds impossible then let me tell you it is not. We know that some businesses can be launched in just 60 hours. That's right, from idea to attracting customers in 2.5 days. The defining factors in achieving this fast result are first to have a clear view, written down, of what success looks like, secondly to set the time frame to achieve that goal and thirdly to define a clear set of steps to get you there. 2.5 days works well for entrepreneurs that have experience of launching start-ups. They know when and where to call upon experts to carry out the tasks that would otherwise be a drain on resources. It would take more than 2.5 days for most people to learn to write code for a website, but a coder will be able to get a site up and running within a couple of hours. The same goes for copy-writing, you may be able to write the content for your website in an evening, but refining the copy may take a few days whereas a copywriter can tighten and add value to your copy in a few hours. Bringing in skills that you do not possess will trim a lot off your timeline. Attempting to do it yourself and then getting frustrated is a false economy. Do what you love and are good at, pay for the rest. That way you can set yourself tight but realistic deadlines and your passion and energy will not fade on the journey due to frustrations. And if you still don't believe us that a business can be created and launched in 2.5 days then read on.

In November 2009, a UK creative agency called Nonsense London put the idea of launching a company at super fast speed to the test, not in 2.5 days, but just 24 hours. They gave themselves 24 hours to conceive, design, build and promote a web-based business. That 24-hour period included everything from them sitting around dreaming up their killer idea to building the website and launching it a day later. The team lived off coffee, pizza and whisky for 24 hours, grabbing some sleep under the desk when they needed it. They wanted to prove how quickly you could devise and launch a business on the web. The result was a business called Dr Hue, a website where you can shop for items by colours; you can read all about how they did it here **24hour-startup.com**. So, if a team of people aided only by pizza and whisky did that in one day, just think what you can do with some decent sleep and 60 times longer.

ZOOM THINKING

1 Focus on your goal, and work backwards.

2 Identify your timeline for how to achieve your goal in 60 days.

3 Don't try and do everything at once. Make sure your goals are manageable.

ZOOM IN ON... JEFFREY KALMIKOFF
'Starting the journey'

Twitter: @jeffrey
Web: callmejeffrey.com

Some people dream about making their spare-room business world famous, and that's exactly what happened with the T-shirt business Threadless. At Threadless.com people upload their T-shirt designs and if they receive enough votes, winning designs are sold online. Jeffrey Kalmikoff helped build the company from a profitable side-project into a multi-million dollar brand with an online community of over a million T-shirt and design enthusiasts.

Jeffrey was Chief Creative Officer at Threadless' parent, skinnyCorp, from 2003 to 2009, went on to become Director of Design & User Experience at Digg, and is now VP of Product at SimpleGeo, based in San Francisco. Alongside his role at Simple Geo, Jeffrey works with start-ups: he's an adviser to the online marketplace Store Envy, to the Mission Bicycle Company, and is a mentor for 500 Startups and TechStars.

Across all that entrepreneurial spirit that he's touched here are Jeffrey's tips for faster, easier ways to make your business idea happen:

1   The best tool an entrepreneur can have is the ability to be honest with themselves about what they are and are not capable of.

2   Setting goals is essential, but the trick is about setting realistic, achievable goals that outline a road-map that gets you from point A to point B.

3   Prototypes are very important, but Jeffrey doesn't see the difference between an early product and a prototype. If it works, get it out there!

4   Don't be your own worst enemy when it comes to taking that first step. You can always adjust your footing depending on the outcome of your first step, but that first step is the most important one you'll take.

LICENCE TO BE *curious*

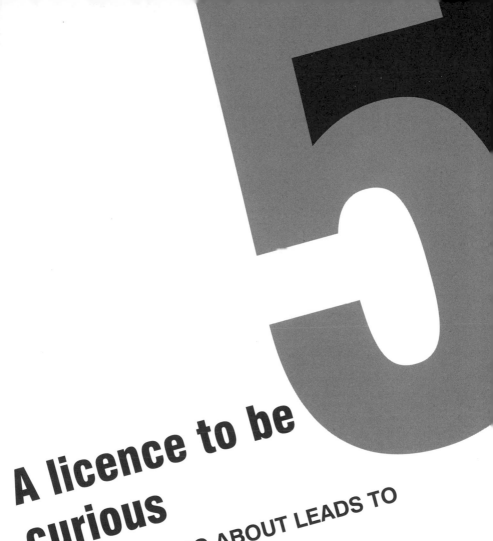

A licence to be curious

HOW SNOOPING ABOUT LEADS TO BUSINESS SUCCESS

Is your business idea nagging away at you? Is it demanding you take some kind of action but you're not sure what to do next? Do you keep on coming back to your idea, in dreams, in the middle of meetings, on your commute to work? If you have an idea that can't be ignored, it's time to get curious and start scratching that itch.

Being curious is about being ready to hear the truth, from many angles surrounding your idea and its journey to launch. It will require a total open mind. You are at the beginning, not the end of your journey so don't suppose or assume anything. As the Buddhist priest, Shunryu Suzuki, said: 'In the beginner's mind there are many possibilities. In the expert's mind there are few.' So embrace the many possibilities.

It's time to understand the pitfalls, opportunities and how to tune your business so that it exactly resonates with your audience. The good news is that it doesn't matter if you don't start out knowing all the answers. We heard the story about a London woman who set up a cakes company without knowing anything about baking. But she went on the Internet and learnt everything she needed to know, watching YouTube videos and practising at home. Now she teaches others how to bake as part of her business.

A licence to be curious will clearly take up lots of time in the early stages as you involve yourself in asking questions and discovering answers that form and shape your business idea. It may seem at first that you can simply Zoom your business into being by skipping the research. Well, the time you invest now being curious, doing that upfront research, before you get the menu printed, will save you time and money later and is often the difference between business success and failure. Being curious now will save assuming too much and potentially getting it wrong.

So when we say 'research' we don't mean you need to sit in the British Library all day, wading through dusty books and documents. Nor will you be sat behind a computer looking at websites all day. It's not boring research, we call it a 'licence to be curious' for a reason, because being curious should be fun. Like

being
curious
should be
fun

when you go away to a new city. You check in to your hotel, and then go for a walk. Sometimes with a map, often without. You'll check out a local coffee shop, spot an interesting bookshop, discover a museum and make a mental note of what you can now be going to do for the rest of the weekend. Those random turns down alleys, finding that shop selling chess sets, that really cool outdoor bar serving amazing tapas under a flowering jacaranda tree – these are the experiences that not just inform your journey, they make it great. And they're no different from business curiosity, having a look around, understanding the landscape and using that new knowledge to your advantage.

As we write this, we're sitting in a Leon restaurant in Spitalfields, east London. It's a nice place to hang out on a winter's afternoon. Looking around we wonder how the founders of Leon arrived at the ideas in their restaurant that we're experiencing right now. Why did they decide to furnish the interior like a European neighbourhood café rather than a bland fast-food joint? Why did they decide to offer meatballs on the menu and gluten free chocolate brownies?

Surely that wasn't the result of some grand formulaic strategy out of the 'How to Build an Alternative Fast-Food Restaurant' handbook; it must have been the result of the owners being curious, asking questions, understanding what people really wanted to eat on a cold winter's day in London. Speaking to the owners we discovered that the Leon experience we are enjoying today came from a whole lot of research. It came from asking potential customers questions about their eating habits, not satisfied with the first round of questions the founder John Vincent engaged in mapping customer types to shape the menu. They used their licence to be curious, dig around, understand what the customer would want, dropped their own assumptions and used all that intelligence to provide a service that people happily pay money for.

What did we do before we started writing this book? We explored. Went for a stroll (quite a long stroll – around Paris), we read numerous articles on the subject of business. We spoke to entrepreneurs of large and small companies and we asked lots of questions. We soaked it all up. It was all pretty random at first – that tends to be the nature of curiosity. No big plan or long to-do list. We'd see where conversations and meetings would take us and then where they would take us next. Some conversations ended up in this book you are reading, some did not. Some articles helped shape our opinions that make the content here, some did not, but everything we read, everyone we interviewed, everything we learnt went to make this book what it is. Had we not bothered to use our licence to be curious this would have been a book filled with only the information about business that we already knew from previous experience. We would have been forced to assume all manner of things to fill the pages.

being curious includes sitting with your laptop on your sofa checking out competitor websites

Investing – and indulging – in being curious includes sitting with your laptop or on your sofa checking out competitor websites. (Check out Chapter 10 where we introduce our 60-Minute Task for getting stuff done.) It could be watching a Do Lecture, a TED Talk or reading an article from a magazine on your chosen field to inspire you. But the real value from being curious comes from going out and about, pounding the streets, spending time face to face really getting to understand your field. Asking lots of questions: of others, of potential customers and competitors.

Sometimes the biggest impact on your research can be gained by 'crossing borders', learning lessons from a completely different industry and don't just restrict yourself to looking at business. Learn lessons in how to stand out or how to communicate from art, street signs and hotel receptionists. Learn how to (or how not to) treat customers from air stewards, shop staff and taxi drivers. There are no rules, you have a licence to be curious and you must use it. Use it to understand the landscape of your business and better ways of delivering it, marketing it and enjoying it. Taking a little longer at a market stall selling T-shirts may seem irrelevant to your business selling software. And then you notice, on selling a T-shirt to a customer, that the stall holder has developed a unique way of gift wrapping the product. It may be beautiful in its simplicity and just what you need as a way of shipping your product. Your previous idea for a packaging solution may have been costly and time consuming and here you are watching a guy who sells T-shirts demonstrate right before your eyes a simple, effective, time saving, money saving beautiful solution. Your licence to be curious means now, once the stall holder has finished serving his customer, you can quiz him about the wrapping. Where did the idea come from, how much is it, where can you buy it? You'll be surprised how forthcoming people are when you pay an interest in what they do.

you have a licence to be curious and you must use it

ZOOM THINKING

1 Start a scrapbook to capture your research.

2 Get out of the house! Talk to people and listen.

3 See how other people are doing things well; be alert to how that can influence your own business.

ZOOM IN ON... JOHN VINCENT

'One foot in the business and one outside it'

Web: leonrestaurants.co.uk

As more people start businesses without needing fixed offices, coffee shops become good places to base yourself. With its free wifi, good coffee and friendly surroundings, Leon restaurants in London have become a popular hangout for people starting out in business. John Vincent co-founded Leon in July 2004 with a mission to change the face of fast food with the single-minded proposition of 'What if God did fast food?' There are now 10 restaurants in London serving healthy fast food to over 50,000 people a week.

People told John he was crazy trying to revolutionise fast food when most people are content with another burger bar or pizza joint. But with careful research they've created a popular destination for Londoners looking for a healthy alternative for fast food.

John's tips for faster, easier ways to make your business idea happen:

1 The key thing is to have one foot in the business and one outside it; you need the foot outside to give you the clarity and the perspective, the foot in is street fighting and doing the right thing.

2 Emotional stability is incredibly important managing the peaks and troughs: don't get too excited when it's a good day, don't get too down when it's a bad day.

3 Have a touchstone, a real simple phrase that guides everything you do. 'What if God did fast food?' really gave Leon a sense of where they'd be in the High Street, what sort of food they'd do. Having that touchstone gives you that crystal-clear thinking.

4 The customer does not know what they want! Steve Jobs said don't listen to the customer as it's not their job to know what they want; they'll only describe it within their current norms.

Video interview with John at **thezoomguys.com**.

Shaping your idea

HOW TO BOX UP YOUR BUSINESS FOR YOUR CUSTOMERS

So you've got your business idea and you're proud of it. Rightly so. Was it a eureka moment for you? Did you take that beermat home and is it taped to the fridge door, your idea captured on a piece of card? Or perhaps your idea's been sitting in that notepad, in that file on your laptop or on that piece of paper on your pin-board?

Now you've got to turn that raw idea into a way to make you money. A product that people will want to buy. It's now time to shape all your thoughts into a clear, simple, compelling proposition. To do that you need to start out by establishing what is the single most compelling benefit that your idea offers the buyer.

PART ONE: WHAT IS THE MOST IMPORTANT BENEFIT YOU HAVE TO OFFER?

the one benefit that stands out above all other benefits that your business idea offers

This summing up of the most important benefit that your business will offer is commonly known as the 'single-minded proposition': *single-minded* because it is focused on just one thought; *proposition* taken from the word proposal. Your single-minded proposition, the declarative sentence, the single most attractive benefit of your business idea. The one benefit that stands out above all other benefits that your business idea offers.

Choosing the single most attractive benefit of your idea, product or service will be difficult, as you probably have identified many benefits. But for this you just need one benefit, the most important one, and it must be the one that is most important to the recipient of your idea, not the one you are most attracted to. What is the problem they have and you are solving for them? You may be tempted to shoehorn in several benefits, but don't or your offering will appear vague.

If you're thinking, 'Yep, I've got it' and your low pricing is your single-minded proposition, some words of warning. Launching a business with the promise of being cheaper than the competition is fine if you own the intellectual property of your idea and therefore competitors can't sell the same product as you. But if you don't, and competitors can match you on price, or even sell their product or service cheaper, you will have two problems. Once you make your proposition based on price, being the cheapest, you will find it difficult to put your price up. Secondly, if your only benefit is 'cheaper than the current competition' and someone figures out a way to deliver the same idea cheaper you will end up having to cut deeper into your profit to beat them. People are happy to pay a little more for what they want, so find a benefit that you can charge a premium for. If you launch an online business selling replacement mobile phone batteries, your benefit for the customer could be that you post the battery for following day delivery. Most people realise they need to buy a new battery when the old one dies, and then they need it in a hurry. You may be £1 more expensive than the 'Cheapest Online Battery Store', but the convenience outweighs the saving. The same could be said for a business that advises companies on tax law. Being the cheapest may produce a negative perception about your professionalism. Cheap ain't always good.

Having a single-minded proposition not only helps the marketplace 'get it'; it also helps drive and motivate you. It will help you focus your efforts when you risk getting sidetracked or distracted.

So now we're going to help you produce your single-minded proposition. Remember it's got to be just one benefit. So here is how you can reach the benefit in three simple steps.

1   What is the problem or headache the consumer had before hearing about your idea?
Answer in a sentence or two.

2   How do you want the customer to react after finding out about your idea? (What will their emotion be?)
Answer in a sentence or two.

3   The proposition is the logical conclusion of the answers you provide from the questions above.

The proposition must…

→ be a rational fact;

→ bring to life the consumer benefit;

→ be single-minded, i.e. one thought;

→ be eight words or less.

So if we were to apply our *Zoom!* book idea to these three steps, it would go something like this.

1   What is the problem the consumer had before hearing about your idea?
Answer: finding the journey to launching a business slow and complicated. Time is money so they would like some techniques that will speed up the process and make it easier.

2   How do you want the customer to react after finding out about your idea?
Answer: They're excited, at last a book that will give them useful tips and techniques so they can launch their business faster and easier.

3   The single-minded proposition: 'a faster way to launch your business' (seven words).

Our book contains more valuable information than just explaining techniques to get your business up and running quickly. But speed is what we identified as being the single most important problem for people trying to launch a business. If it takes someone a year to launch their business, then the idea may wither on the vine, starved of time and funds. For a business to succeed you need to act quickly, whilst the idea is motivating you. So the main focus of our book is speed of launching a business. Not how to cut corners or cheat, but how to adopt a mindset of speed and techniques to take the business from your mind to making money as quickly as possible. So every sentence, every paragraph, every chapter we write, we get to ask, is this related to helping people just like you get their business up and running in the fastest time possible?

Leon, the London-based fast-food chain, have as their single-minded proposition: 'If God did fast food'.

The proposition enables the restaurant chain to focus: every day they can always ask the simple question, is what they are doing today in line with their proposition? Imagine there's a trend that sweeps the nation for deep-fried cup cakes; would Leon start stocking them? No – it doesn't fit with 'If God did fast food' (there's no deep frying in God's kitchen). So unless they could find a way of giving this a Godly spin, you won't find it on the menu.

So work out your proposition: define it and get it tattooed on your arm. In a crowded, abundant market packed with similar offerings, the only way you can differentiate yourself is by having a single-minded proposition, one of value to your customers, and sticking to it.

PART TWO: DESCRIBE YOUR BUSINESS IN 140 CHARACTERS OR LESS

Now you have described the single most important benefit it's time for you to expand the thought. Just over so slightly. You need to explain what the idea is in 120 characters or less. 140 characters is the length of a tweet, but for someone to retweet your message, to send it to their followers, you will need to allow 20 spare characters. If you don't, they will need to edit your message and they may just edit out an important part. So 120 characters (including spaces) is all you have to explain what you do or what your product is. Once you can explain your offering in this tight space, you will be able to describe it to any prospect without them getting lost in the detail. And that's important. Clarity. Keep It simple. Complexity is overrated.

To get to those precious 120 characters you will need to start by answering the following:

1 Who is your audience?
   Answer this question in a sentence.

2 What headache or problem does your idea solve?
   Answer this question in a sentence. You may find that your single-minded proposition will work here.

3 Why should the customer care about your product?
   Answer this question in a sentence

4 What is your point of difference?
   Answer this question in a sentence. You may find your single-minded proposition will work here.

Once again, if we were to apply *Zoom!* the book to the above, it would look something like this.

1 Who is your audience?
   Answer: all kinds of people with business ideas that really want to launch them.

2 What headache or problem does your idea solve?
   Answer: the headache of trying to launch a business.

3 Why should the customer care about your product?
   Answer: we have included techniques that make the journey faster.

4 What is your point of difference?
   Answer: we offer a faster way to launch a business.

Our Twitter message:

New book out now called *Zoom!* It's packed with great ideas for people who want to launch a business quickly. (108 characters, leaving room for a short link to our website!)

Remember, brevity wins here: the simpler your offering can be communicated the better. Nailing the description in 140 characters is not just about Twitter, it's bigger than that, it's your proposition in a nutshell, your elevator pitch and that brevity is critical for websites, business cards, getting other people to refer your business and general clarity of mind.

nailing the description in 140 characters is your proposition in a nutshell

Later on you may want to adjust these descriptions, but right now they are your magnets. Ask of everything you do towards making your business happen this simple question – does it stick to my 120 character description here? If it does, you are moving forward; if it does not, then you may be sidetracked.

So is your idea feeling more real now, is it beginning to take shape? Can you explain your business idea to Auntie Beth over a glass of wine in a busy restaurant without her glazing over? Good. The power of being able to articulate your idea with ease and confidence will enable others to have confidence in you. So practise repeating your single-minded proposition until it is second nature and do the same with your 120-character description.

PART THREE: MAKING YOUR IDEA BOXABLE

Now for the final stage of realising your idea, taking your idea from your dream to reality, we are going to put your business in a box. It needs to be boxable. Of course, your product may be something quite intangible, like a digital offering or it may be a consultancy business where your product is know-how. That doesn't sound very boxable, does it? But customers prefer concrete offerings over abstract notions, they get boxes. So whatever it is you make, whatever your product might be, wrap it into a box, stick a label on it and put it on a shelf with a nice big bow on it.

The box will be what your customers will see, pick up, inspect, and decide if they want to buy what you have to offer. This exercise is not a test of your design skills. This is not a test of how well you can design a box to go into retail outlets. Your box can, and it should, look pretty raw and unglamorous because this is a test of what messages and images mixed together will persuade people to buy your product or service. And like the exercises that helped you define your proposition and explain what you do in 120 characters this test will enable you to see your offer for the first time. You will be able to see what you are selling and that visualisation of your business will help you explain the benefits to others. It will also act as a kind of anchor, keeping you from drifting away from your business idea. You will be able to take one look at your box and ask yourself 'Is what I am doing today adding value to selling what's in the box?'

So let's box up your business for customers; any old box will do. A cereal box is always good. Now wrap it crudely in plain paper so you have a blank box. Now in big letters in the top third of the front of the box write a headline based on your proposition.

Here is some help in writing headlines. There are only three types of headline. There is the 'promise', i.e. **Bald? Grow new hair today**. There is the 'news', i.e. new and interesting – **Man lands on Mars**. And there is the 'intrigue', i.e. **Man bites dog**.

The job of the headline is to tease enough of the story that the reader wants to know more.

So the *Zoom!* single-minded proposition is 'Zoom! The faster way to make your business idea happen'.

visualisation of your business will help you explain the benefits to others

As a promise headline we could write something like: '*New book offers a faster way to launch your business*'. We have promised the person who picks up the box that the contents will help them launch their business quickly. If that is what they are shopping for, if that is the problem they are trying to solve, then they will probably read more of the messages on the box to make sure that what's inside really is for them. Alternatively, if the *Zoom!* message were written as a news headline it could read: '*Latest techniques for launching a business quickly*'. And if the headline were written as an intrigue, it might read like this: '*How to launch a business in 60 days*'.

Keep your headline direct, clear and to the point. Cut out any unnecessary words, fluff or filler and don't be vague or woolly with your language. Avoid puns, words that require a dictionary reference to understand and made up words. Think plain English.

To test your headline we want you to imagine that you are leaning out of a second-floor window just as a motorcycle pulls up at a traffic light on the road below you. You have just a few seconds before the lights change and the motorcycle will disappear into the distance. You want to inform the rider as to what your business offers. So we would shout out the headline 'New book offers a faster way to launch your business'. Does the motorcyclist understand what we're offering?

Next you will need a few lines of copy that will go underneath the headline to explain what your product or service does. The customer was attracted to your headline, now they need to know more. Try and view the purpose of your offering from a customer perspective. How will it make their life better, easier, faster? So, again, using the *Zoom!* book headline 'New book offers a faster way to launch your business' the text underneath, in a smaller font could read: 'Is launching your business feeling like a slow process?

Does it feel like you may run out of time and money before the cash starts flowing? Are you wondering "what's next" as you navigate the muddy waters of a business start-up? If you have answered yes to any of the above, then this book is for you. *Zoom! The Faster Way to Make Your Business Idea Happen* is packed with powerful tools and techniques that will help you get your business up and running quickly.' You may recognise this statement; it's the first paragraph of the Introduction.

Now you have a headline and an explanation of your business you will need an image. People process visual information 600,000 times faster than text, so the image you choose will catch the eye of your shopper faster than the headline will. To choose your image you will need to take your single-minded proposition, in our case 'Zoom! The faster way to make your business idea happen' and dramatise it as an image. Again, this is not a test of your creativity or ability to draw. This is an exercise in making your business idea come to life and feel real, it is a chance for you to adjust it, tweak it, change it and understand it before you commit to it. It will save you precious time later as you will be quite definite as to exactly what your business is. You will be surprised how many new business start-ups really can't articulate what they are actually offering! They waste time doing things that are not directly connected to getting their business up and running. So back to the *Zoom!* single-minded proposition and how we could dramatise it as an image. 'Zoom! The faster way to make your business idea happen'. This could be shown as a shop flying up into space powered by a rocket. Not particularly creative, but it makes the point, and that's all we want to do is make the point. So we have a headline, an image and now we need to add some messaging to the box. It could be an imaginary testimonial, what would you like customers

people process visual information faster than text, so the image you choose will catch the eye of your shopper faster than the headline

to say about your product? For example 'This book really helped me focus on getting my business started fast'. Or 'I thought it would take me a year to start my business but after reading this book I was up and running in two months'. You may want to add some bullet points describing the benefits of your business idea. Using this book as an example again, it could look something like this:

→ The book that will help you get your business off the ground quickly.

→ Simple to follow, proven techniques that will save you time.

→ No previous business experience necessary.

Finally, you will need to consider where you will add the price. Is it a feature (great value), a little sticker on the bottom of the box or by application only?

Now you have your business idea in a box. For the first time it is physical. You can look at it. You can share it with your prospects and get feedback. If your creative talents leave a little to be desired you can keep it for yourself as a reminder of what the most important messages around your business are. But don't spend precious time perfecting it, the true purpose of this exercise is to realise the benefits of your business.

ZOOM THINKING

1 What is the most important benefit your business offers?

2 Describe your business in 140 characters or less.

3 How are you going to make your idea boxable?

---

6 SHAPING YOUR IDEA

Imagine it
HOW TO BE A VISIONARY

Can you imagine making your first sale? If not, then you have a problem; because your ability to visualise such milestones will act as a floodlight to illuminate your business idea first in your mind and then in the real world. That's why they call entrepreneurs visionaries, because they have vision – they can draw a mental picture of what it is they intend to do and then when they see it working in their mind, they go to work to build it in the real world.

When we put our imagination to use we can see what it is we want to achieve before we spend time and money actually building it. We can tune and adjust the model in our minds until we deem the idea fit for purpose. So it's time to leverage your imagination.

Novelist and business storyteller Preethi Nair told us that whether it was turning her ideas into books or setting up a business, she always had a vision of what she wanted to achieve. When she was writing her books she had this vision of seeing them in the bookstore on the shelf under the letter 'N'; with the business she had an idea of the type of clients she wanted to work with. Preethi acknowledged that she's always had a sense of what she wants to do, but never knows how she's going to do it. 'All I know is that I dream, I take one step towards the dream and then I rely on all the things you can't manufacture like serendipity, coincidence, meeting people and then I allow that to take me where I'm supposed to go.' That visualisation, that dream enables her to make the idea happen.

In Chapter 14, 'Magic Umbrella', we will explain how the subconscious mind can't tell the difference between what we imagine and what is real. We tell the story of Dan being called into his boss's office, how he assumed he'd done something wrong, subsequently experiencing a physical reaction to what he was imagining in his mind. The takeout from Dan's story is that our subconscious mind can't tell the difference between what we imagine and what is actuality. When we imagine something happening, it is exactly the same as it happening. Drawing a mental picture, imagining it, can therefore be a powerful tool for you to exploit when it comes to getting your business launched quicker. If you can visualise your website, page by page, clicking through the content, then you will be able to articulate your requirements to your designer and save time and money on redesigns. If

drawing a mental picture can be a powerful tool to exploit when it comes to getting your business launched quicker you can visualise a customer browsing through your shop, then you will be able to lay it out so that it is the best customer experience possible. If you visualise the problem your new software will solve and see it working, then the coding will be able to happen faster as you will know exactly what you need the code to do.

If you can't visualise it, you might get stuck. Ian was working on a complex report for a client, there was a lot of data to wade through and it was proving to be really difficult. How could he process all that disparate information into a single compelling report. Then Ian noticed he started to visualise that final report: a 10-page PDF with a couple of diagrams, a simple title, some headings in red. He could even see the page numbers. And then: 'Zoom!', he got unstuck. His mental block vanished as he could understand what he needed to do. Building that report became a fast execution of what he could see in his mind.

So what tips can we give you to help you visualise? For some it comes easy, for others you may need a little practice. The good news is that you won't even need to sit in a classroom to get good at this. You can do it anywhere and no one will ever know that you are practising.

To start you will need to think of a problem or challenge. Let's say you decide to make a video for your website that explains how your product or service works. You have written a script and filming is due to take place in one week's time. This gives you plenty of time to create a mental picture of your video, to see yourself reading that script, acting out your part. Then you check to 'see' and 'hear' if firstly the script flows well and explains enough about your business and secondly if you do a good job of imparting the information to your audience. The act of being able to view your video before you go in to production will serve you well on two fronts. Firstly, you can spot any potential problems with the script and secondly it will help calm your nerves on the day. If you imagine yourself doing a great job of delivering your script, your subconscious mind will believe that there is nothing to worry about and will be less likely to raise fears on the day.

An ideal way to practise visualisation is to find somewhere quiet, turn off your phone and relax. All kinds of unrelated thoughts might fill your mind – don't worry, that is perfectly normal. Just give yourself permission to push them out of your mind as soon as they interrupt you. Make sure you start each session with a clear goal; having a desire for the outcome at the start will ensure you don't end up flipping from one thought to another, a bit like grazing through TV channels. Now begin to think about what it is you need to visualise. If you have trouble bringing the image to mind try imagining that you are sitting in a big comfortable chair, you have a remote control in your hand and in front of you is a large screen TV. Now let's take the example of creating a video for your website. It doesn't matter that you don't know the script verbatim, for now you just want to see how you look on the TV, see yourself walking and talking and looking comfortable with it. This gives you time to see the detail too, things like what's in the background, what are you wearing, the body language you are projecting and is it right for the video? You may even remember part of the script so press pause on your remote control. Now practice saying the lines you can remember once in your head and then when you are ready, press play. Now you can watch and listen as you perform your script. Repeating this many times gives you a chance to watch the performance as a viewer, you get to see your body language, hear the script and make changes that will improve the final product. You will also get to know which parts of the script you are struggling with and either practise it further or adjust the wording of the script so that it is easier to recall.

This technique is used by professionals all over the world in every aspect of business. It can be practised in downtime; it's free; it enables you to pre-problem solve as well as adding to your confidence. The technique can be used in a delivery of a presentation, advising a customer or the development of a software solution.

By visualising what you want you are also instructing your mind to be alert to that element. You know how it is when you buy a new car, suddenly it seems that the roads are full of the same car? Of course, we know they have always been there, but your mind has become aroused to them and notices them now where as previously they were ignored. So in the past your new car passed you by unnoticed, but it was always there and now you see it, standing out from the crowd. The same can be said for business solutions. You may never have met a web developer, and now you need one. But the truth is that you have probably met more than one web developer who has actually told you that they are a web developer. But at the time it didn't register. Your mind said 'Internet person' and moved on. Now you need one. So now, by thinking about what it is you need, your mind will go to work looking for the solution. Then if you randomly meet someone and they so much as mention the word website, your focus will move to that word and you will steer the conversation to find out if they can recommend a web developer to you.

There's another way you can leverage your mind to help your business: via another technique straight out of the therapy room, it is called the Miracle Question. It is a way of getting you, your customer or prospect to visualise what it is they really want and explain it to you clearly. It is especially useful for projects where ambiguity could exist or a reluctance for the client to enlighten you. Using the Miracle Question can really speed up your process for launching your business. By asking your client the Miracle Question you will be

another technique straight out of the therapy room is called the Miracle Question armed with a clear understanding of what they actually want. That way you can finely tune your business to precisely resonate with your prospects' needs.

Here is the Miracle Question: we're going to give you a magic wand, with that you can change whatever you want. So you use it, and when you wake up tomorrow morning and it worked, everything is just how you wanted it to be. Tell me, what has changed?

The Magic Wand is about unlocking answers and getting clarity through visualisation. By giving the prospect a chance to focus on the solution free from the constraints of what in their mind is or is not possible, you will arrive at a clear need.

The Magic Wand levers the power of your imagination to fix business challenges. You can carry it around in your virtual toolkit. And when you get stuck, when you need to get clarity from the muddle, when you need to unlock your own creativity or drill down to establish your customer's needs, get it out and wave it around. Knowing a potential customer's need before you pitch your product means you can shape your business to fit their needs.

So whether it's using the Magic Wand and asking the Miracle Question or visualising your business idea launching, leveraging your imagination is a powerful tool in making your business idea happen faster. As soon as you've visualised something, you've made a commitment; you're on the road to making it real. Seeing in your mind how your dream can turn into reality is really powerful. Like the recollection of that vivid dream you had last night, it feels so real, and that kind of reassurance can make what you thought was daunting and even impossible seem very possible and within your grasp. That emotional investment can make a fundamental difference in success. You need to know what success looks like for you. After all, how can you hit a target if you don't know what it looks like?

the Magic
Wand
is about
unlocking
answers
and getting
clarity
through
visualisation

ZOOM THINKING

1 Start making visualisation part of your business thinking.

2 Visualise your goal. Get very familiar with how it looks and feels.

3 Think how the Miracle Question can help you understand what your customers want.

Think like a speedboat

LESSONS IN AGILITY

When you're launching a business it is a fact that things will go wrong. That's not a criticism, it's not because of sloppiness. It's just life. That's why you need to think like a speedboat. Be agile, be quick, be able to change direction in an instant. Because if you don't, your business will be so rigid, you won't have the ability to rapidly respond to changing trends or react fast enough to your customers.

One morning at a meeting with the fashion brand, Benetton, Ian was asked whether he could introduce them to a London advertising agency – Benetton wanted to place an ad in the *Evening Standard* newspaper later that week about a new store opening. Ian telephoned a couple of contacts he had in agencies thinking they would be delighted to work with a brand like Benetton. Both agencies told Ian to tell Benetton that they would be more than happy to come in and talk to them next week, sit down, work out their goals and plan a campaign. This 'supertanker approach', slow to react to the opportunity, gave Ian an idea. He called a designer friend, hired a copywriter and in a couple of phone calls struck a deal with a media buying company that could buy Ian space in the *Evening Standard*. Later that day Ian was standing in the queue at his local bank ready to transfer money into the media buyer's account to secure the ad booking. Ian delivered where traditional agencies could not. He thought like a speedboat; as a result he secured a lucrative relationship with the brand and they got their advert out on time. That's the power of thinking like a speedboat.

That mindset does not come easily, especially if you have been working within a large company and are used to a life of constant conference calls, hour long face to face meetings followed by a string of emails and finally a decision being made only after everyone has written a detailed PowerPoint deck on the subject. But this speedboat mentality is what's required for your very survival in business, and that thinking will go a long way to your success. When a brick wall appears in front of you, when the sky falls in, when it feels like it's all going wrong, the ability to change tact quickly to navigate around the problem is essential. The corporate world will be busy seeking permission from each layer of management whilst you, the entrepreneur, can make decisions that make an instant positive difference.

Instagram is a photo manipulation app for the iPhone. It became enormously successful in late 2010, just a few weeks after launching, as a result of becoming Apple's App of the Week. Their users reached over half a million in their first month. TechCrunch.com reported that co-founders Kevin Systrom and Mike Krieger initially launched a similar product called Burbn but once they had it live it felt cluttered and over-run with features. So they took the brave move of ditching it. They quickly rethought the whole offering through again. Every detail from top to bottom, nothing too sacred to be scrapped, and just eight weeks later Instagram was born. That was a critical change in direction that only a speedboat mindset could make and it enabled Kevin and Mike to create success. We can see from the story just how easy it would have been for the two of them to try and tweak the product a little or insist nothing is wrong with it and blame poor user numbers on everything other than the truth that stared them in the face and ultimately miss the opportunity to achieve success. Instead, in just eight weeks, they had a new product, rethought from the ground up with the user in mind, fit for purpose and destined to bring Kevin and Mike fame and fortune. Thinking like a speedboat gives you the ability to rethink, redesign, react to the market and meet the demands of customers.

So to make your business idea happen you need to stay flexible, agile and open-minded. That way, when a Monday morning email arrives with news of a competitor that threatens to totally disrupt your service and turn your business on its head, you take it all in your stride. You say 'OK, let's be ready to change tack if we have to'. Changing tack is not a weakness, it's obligatory in this fast moving world that we live in. Having the mindset to embrace that is key, otherwise when that realisation hits you that you need to rethink

changing tack is not a weakness, it's obligatory in this fast moving world

you'll be getting emotional and making bad decisions, or, you'll give up.

When Richard Moross launched the first iteration of a company that would develop into the business card company Moo.com, it failed. Fell flat on its face. One reason was because it had completely the wrong name – 'Pleasure Cards'. It was the rejection of that first iteration and the lessons learnt that led to his ultimate success. Richard could never have planned for that failure. He didn't know it would happen. But by thinking flexibly and reacting to changing trends, Moo.com was born.

Richard told us that the business started as a partner-based business, working with Flickr as their print partner. That focus made sense as Richard did not think that any of their customers would want to load designs or pictures direct to their site. But a few months in they decided to launch an uploader so people could upload designs for a business card direct. That caused what Richard describes as a:

Huge change to the business. We thought we would be 90% partner based and it was the opposite – 10% partner based, 90% direct because we were creating a brand and the relationship with the customer. So it was a massive tactical change and we had no foresight there.

small shifts in strategy or product development have a massive impact in the marketplace

Those pivots can be such small shifts in strategy or product development, yet they have a massive impact in the marketplace with consumers. They can turn a missable idea into something unmissable. Entrepreneurial businesses have advantages over larger competitors as they can adapt and change by being nimble and quick. They can listen to the customer, realise a truth and then change direction – just like that – without getting stuck in structure, process and bureaucracy. That is the competitive advantage.

At our 'Unplan Your Business' panel discussion in Texas we asked a room full of business owners how many had written a business plan. Just about every hand went up. We than asked how many of those people had looked at the plan since they wrote it. About a quarter of the hands went up. Then we asked how many people had looked at the plan in the last year. Not many hands went up at all. It quickly became apparent through the conversation that followed that the entrepreneurs in the room had mostly written a plan because they believed that is what they were expected to do as a business start-up. Further questioning also brought to life the fact that most of those start-ups had pitched for funding, and although most had submitted a business plan, those that received the funding didn't believe that the business plan had any bearing on the funding (mostly because they felt that the original plan was quite removed from the offering they were pitching due to adjusting their business tack during their journey but not rewriting the plan to suit).

So we encourage you to have goals in mind, but we don't suggest you have a fixed linear route for how you're going to get there. How many opportunities in your life have arisen randomly or serendipitously? How many of us found our clients by some random meeting in a bar, got that eureka moment from staying in the shower two minutes longer than usual, stumbled upon that link by spotting a blink-and-you'll-miss-it tweet? Similarly, how many of us met our partners in the same way? That's how life works. And that's how your business will develop. You need to develop a mentality that embraces and celebrates those kind of opportunities, rather than rejects them.

We spoke to Tony Hsieh, the CEO of online retailer Zappos. Zappos has been a great success story of how a company selling shoes grew a business based on providing awesome customer service; its turnover

> **have goals in mind but don't have a fixed linear route for how you're going to get there**

topped $1 billion in 2008 and the next year was acquired by Amazon in a deal worth around $880 million. We asked Tony for his take on business agility:

> *Charles Darwin said, 'It is not the strongest of the species that survives, nor the most intelligent that survives. It is the one that is the most adaptable to change.' At Zappos, we believe the same is true for business.*

So if you're looking to build a billion-dollar business, adaptability wins. Indeed, your ability to adapt quickly and efficiently could be the critical difference between failure and success. So strip back to basics, keep it simple and lose the baggage. You need a supertanker to carry lots of baggage, a speedboat suffers when you overload it.

ZOOM THINKING

1 Agility wins, so be ready for rapid change.

2 Re-tune your business thinking to embrace serendipity.

3 Remember, you're a speedboat now, so there's no room for baggage. So don't bring it onboard.

Embrace business doing

THE POWER OF GETTING STUFF DONE

Go to your library, bookshop or online bookstore and see just how many books you can find under '*business planning*'. You'll find volumes and volumes of books on how to write a business plan. Now have a look at books on '*business doing*'. You won't find many. In fact, you may not find any. That's because the rules of business put more emphasis and importance on planning than on doing.

We think that's crazy. The trouble with business planning is that you can make yourself very busy just plotting the future, trying to work out every possible eventuality, playing with endless 'what ifs'. Keeping yourself busy writing plans may make you think you're being productive. But is it the fastest way to launch your business? Planning is not doing. Success is achieved by those very few that are busy doing, not writing down an endless list of things they should do.

So many people talk about doing stuff: 'My new website is going to be awesome, it's just that it's going through its third design concept so won't be ready for a while'. 'My new shop isn't going to open yet because we haven't decided what colour the counter will be and until we can make our minds up it's going to hold everything up'. 'Yes, we will be tweeting and blogging about our new business but first we just need to produce a social media strategy document'. Sounds familiar? Too many perfectly reasonable people obsess about the details of what they're planning to do at the risk of neglecting the most important word in the entrepreneur's vocabulary: implementation!

the most important word in the entrepreneur's vocabulary: implementation

It's more effective to do stuff than talk about it. It's more productive to lean into the problem and fix it than it is to write a document outlining possible solutions. We live and work in a world where you can launch a website or a blog overnight; it's better having some presence for your new business than no presence at all. You can see the efforts of your labour and adjust it to make it better much faster than you can write a spec sheet. Without a focus on business doing, your business idea will be in danger of staying on a piece of paper and never seeing the light of day. But we still see so many business owners that get caught up in process and procedure that the business project stalls. Think how powerful it is to cut through all the procrastination, ditch the unnecessary procedure and aim to deliver results instead.

In the next chapter, 'Salami steps', we'll introduce you to our super fast way to make decisions in 60 seconds. You write the problem down. Just a sentence will do. Then you give yourself just 60 seconds to make the decision. Yes or no? Green or red background? Charge £5 or £7 per unit? Make the decision and stick with it until either it stays forever or more insight comes into your world and you can see clearly the benefits of changing it.

We spoke to investor Fred Wilson who made the following observation in his blog:

> *People ask me all the time about the traits I look for in entrepreneurs and action orientation is at the top of the list. I'd much rather back someone who makes 100 decisions a day and gets 51 of them right than someone who makes one decision a day and gets it right.*

So stop comparing every business card design and just go ahead and choose one, right now. Stop moving that logo around the web page, leave it to the web designer, it will be fine. You now have permission to get on with the important stuff that will actually get your business in a condition to make money. Stop spending days drafting a customer survey, when you can produce something in a couple of hours using free online tools. Otherwise you will be in danger of procrastinating and delaying your business forever.

Can you see, it's much better to go for the fast launch of your business, to do something proactive right now rather than spend precious time on things that can either wait or are not essential to getting your business up and running. So never underestimate the power of just taking action, however small, to bring you success. It's so incredibly simple, yet so effective.

never underestimate the power of just taking action to bring you success

Kevin Roberts, CEO Worldwide at Saatchi & Saatchi offered us this advice for anyone looking to make their idea happen: '*Execute relentlessly to win... avoid moderation. Focus on every last detail. Personally*'. We'd agree with Kevin on execution but just make sure that focusing on every last detail does not delay your launch. You need to be focused on action.

these tools are game changers making every aspect of business doing more accessible for everyone and in an instant

If you mix a 'just get on with it' mindset with some of the web-based tools that are available, then you can apply business doing to really fast-track your idea. Want to crowd-source suggested names for your new product? Social media will do it in an instant. Want to create a web presence overnight? Free online tools will make that possible. Need to market your website rapidly? It's back to social media. These tools are game changers making every aspect of business doing more accessible for everyone and in an instant too. Many of us take them for granted but they are changing the way we do business and we all need to embrace the value they offer.

Will King told us how Twitter has fast-tracked his ability to talk to the market about new King of Shaves' products. When his new razor was launched, he used Twitter to spread the word and established one-to-one relationships with consumers who were buying and experiencing it. The Internet is packed with quality free tools that are the perfect tools for the business-doer.

This book was made possible by free Internet tools. We used Google Docs that enables multiple people to collaborate on a project. The document that became this book wasn't stored on our local hard drives, instead it is stored on a remote server. They call these remote servers cloud computing. The cloud worked for us writing this book, it meant that either of us could access any part of the book at any time. It revolutionised the process of two people writing a book and meant we could create, write and update documents simultaneously. Sometimes we were in different continents working on the same chapter at the same time. We could see in real time what each other was doing, no waiting for one of us to email the latest version through. Without collaborative working can you just imagine the tens of different versions of files being shared by email with all that margin for error? The writing process would have been slowed down. There would have been no Saturday morning impromptu phone calls discussing revisions for a chapter. No Ian writing a section whilst David is reading the copy as it flows in to place in real time. Adding thoughts and making changes. It would have taken so much longer – and a lot of different font colours! – to achieve the same results without cloud computing. That solution applied to businesses where teams can collaborate across disciplines and timezones on files or where companies can rent server space on a pay as you go basis has accelerated launch times. It's revolutionised businesses, creating services that entrepreneurs can access instantly (and often free).

If you can launch your business quicker, with less time and less people, it means you need less money up front to see if the new business will fly.

Business 'doing-tools' like web apps, cloud computing and social media create a real level playing field for businesses. Suddenly you have the same opportunities on Twitter as the largest global competitor in your field has on the same platform. Online tools can accelerate your own ability and desire to make your idea happen because they have instant, trackable and tangible results.

So the key to business doing is to take that first step and get your idea out there. Launch as cost effectively as possible, as Jeffrey Kalmikoff told us: 'The first step is the most important one you'll take. It's the difference between doing or not – planning a journey is not the same as starting one.'

ZOOM THINKING

1 Rethink your schedule tomorrow. How can you shift focus so you're spending as much time as possible Doing?

2 What Doing-Tools can you introduce to fast track your business?

3 Are you making a big dent in your to-do list?

ZOOM IN ON... FRED WILSON
'I used it and loved it'

Twitter: @fredwilson

Web: avc.com

If you're seeking investment for your business idea, getting insight into what investors are looking for is critical. Fred Wilson is the legendary, New York-based venture capitalist who was an early investor in Twitter. Fred helps start and build technology companies. He is Managing Partner of two venture capital firms, Flatiron Partners and Union Square Ventures, whose investments include Etsy, Foursquare, Meetup, Tumblr and Twitter.

Fred's a busy guy but we emailed him five quick questions; here's what he said back:

1   Q. Would you say most of the good tech ideas were very much 'unfinished' at launch; that their success is about adapting to user feedback?
    Fred: 'Yes, that is why I like the "launch early and often" methodology.'

2   Q. Do you think too many entrepreneurs complicate their ideas: develop a product with too many benefits, with a complicated model, when they just need to keep it simple?
    Fred: 'Yes, very much so.'

3   Q. From all those ideas that land in your in-box, what criterion does it need to pass to get looked at?
    Fred: 'It needs to be an idea I am passionate about.'

4   Q. What are the key traits you look for in entrepreneurs and start-up teams?
    Fred: 'Creativity and tenacity.'

5   Q. So what was it about Twitter that you thought, yep, this is a good idea?
    Fred: 'I used it and loved it.'

10

Salami steps

HOW TO MAKE YOUR BUSINESS HAPPEN SLICE BY SLICE

Now you've worked out your goal you may well feel totally overwhelmed by all the steps you need to navigate to get you from Idea to Launch. Where do you start? And the answer is you start with just ONE step, with one item on your to-do list, one task at a time.

Don't treat your journey as one huge impossible task, take it slice by slice, like you'd slice a salami and oh, if you're vegetarian, try parmesan :) Taking it slice-by-slice means you can segment a huge project or challenge into many thin, easily manageable slices.

First you need to plot your salami steps from idea to reality. Keep it simple, try using a marker pen and a pack of Post-its. Post-it Note mapping has long been used by entrepreneurs for working out a fast simple route to launch their ideas. James Barlow is a Brit who works at the National Collegiate Inventors and Innovators Alliance in the US, an organisation that supports technology innovation and entrepreneurship. We met James at the start of our journey back in Texas; he told us how Post-it Notes have helped people create action plans, making the abstract concrete, translating a complex proposition into something simple.

Clear your kitchen table and on the left hand side put a Post-it with the word 'Idea' on it, and on the right hand side put one with the word 'Launch' on it. You can then play around with a chain of Post-it Notes across the table plotting the different steps and actions required to reach your goal. Remember, nothing's set in stone, you can always unpeel a Post-it and throw it away, insert a new one or change the order. You can come back to it after you have had some time to dwell on the path you have created and evolve it. You won't nail it in one kitchen table session, so you might have to eat breakfast somewhere else for a few days.

Before we started writing *Zoom!*, we took an inspiration trip to Paris where we came up with the structure and ideas that you're now reading. Post-it Notes helped us map out the ideas; we literally couldn't have achieved the same results without them. We used them to salami-slice the project. Without knowing where we were going, we were able to have a start point, and an end point, and then all we had to do was fill out the middle. OK 'the middle' might have taken us the biggest time but Post-its allowed us to brain-dump, move stuff around, and test ideas whilst being able to be flexible. It didn't matter what we said or in what order, because everything is movable and restickable. So on a table on our Eurostar train, on a wall in our Paris apartment, we stuck Post-it Notes, plotting and re-plotting a journey from idea (the concept for a book) to reality (a published book).

If we hadn't brain dumped all our thoughts and organised them into chapters and pointers, we may have suffered writer's block later. And writer's block is the same as entrepreneur's block. It all becomes so daunting and overwhelming you just don't know how to move forward. Even breaking your project down into salami steps can still leave you in a position where one of the steps is holding you up. The longer you remain stuck on this step so the risk of losing your passion increases and failure seems inevitable.

THE 60-MINUTE TASK

So let's take our salami thinking and add a time limit to create our super fast way to work through a large project – the 60-Minute Slice Rule.

Most slices of the salami can be achieved in 60 minutes or less of fully applied effort. They may take longer if you let them, but by giving them a fixed time limit, you will be forced to get them done. The 60-minute approach makes the impossible, possible.

That may sound like a gimmick, but it's not. Sixty minutes to completing a task works like this. Start by breaking your project down in to a list of tasks you need to complete to reach your goal, these are salami steps. Before you go to sleep at night get your head around the next task and what the deliverable

the 60-minute approach makes the impossible, possible.

is, focus on it and think about it for just long enough to isolate it from the other tasks. Viewing it at night allows the problem of how best to solve it to ferment in your mind whilst you sleep. When you come back to the task the following day your brain has already had an opportunity to play with the problem, understand it and try to figure out the easiest way to solve it or complete it. That's what our minds are good at doing, figuring out the best way to do stuff. We've been doing it since the beginning of time. Your mind is tuned to solve problems and figure out the quickest way to complete a task. Need to make fire? Rub two sticks together. Need to chop wood? Fashion an axe. Must keep warm? Remove an animal skin. Need to go into space...? You get the idea.

The following day you set aside one hour in which you will complete the task. The first five minutes of your hour is spent visualising in your mind you actually doing the task from beginning to end. You can imagine this at any speed you want, as long as you are seeing yourself actually doing it. The purpose of this day dreaming is so you can pre problem solve, spot any problems before you get to them. For example, David wanted to build a kitchen. He'd never done this before and owned just one screwdriver and no other tools. David started by stripping out the old kitchen and clearing the space so he could see it. He drew up a list of all the things he would need to buy and another list of tasks. As soon as he got home from work he would visualise doing the task, noticing that he would need a particular tool, or would need help to hold something in place. Five minutes of seeing himself do the job gave him the confidence to do it. The next 45 minutes he would work hard to get the job done. Then after 45 minutes he'd stop and make a cup of tea. The job was either completed or bigger than anticipated and would require dividing up in to another salami step. Either way, David built the kitchen.

So why 60 minutes, why five minutes visualising and why only 45 minutes work? OK the 10 minutes for a cup of tea everyone understands but why the other two? Well, as we saw in Chapter 7, 'Imagine It', when you visualise, you can bend time, you can speed it up to quickly get you through the easy stuff. Or you can slow time down to see clearly how to tackle the more difficult tasks in detail. With the task of building David's kitchen he didn't need to visualise putting in each screw, he could just jump over that process to see it as all the screws in place, a bit like 'here's one we made earlier'. So that is why we visualise 45 minutes' work in just five minutes. It's all that's required to get a good sense of the task ahead. When it is only five minutes of visualisation we have no excuse for letting our minds wander off topic and thinking of other things. As we only have five minutes we must stay focused.

Forty-five minutes is a perfectly good duration for getting on with some serious doing because like the salami steps it is small enough not to intimidate. And in an age where distractions are in abundance it is short enough that you can focus hard to get it done and put off distraction until you have completed.

Chunking it down puts goals, productivity and a sense of achievement within reach; it's about breaking down the task in to manageable chunks. Sixty minutes, five minutes visualisation, 45 doing and 10 for a cup of tea just gives you a memorable framework to get stuff done quickly.

Putting it into practice for launching your own business could look like this: You need to do research about the kind of accessories people buy in a mobile phone shop? Imagine yourself for five minutes visiting mobile phone shops, asking the staff questions, taking notes. Then you dive in, go on an inspiration trip to the High Street or the shopping mall, soak it up, live and breathe it for 45 minutes of absolute focused attention. You will come back with notes, ideas and answers. Alternatively, you need to understand potential competition for a business online. You can track down quite a few businesses in a 45 minute fully focused session, right? You can spend the first five visualising tracking down competitors. Visualising the kind of words you will need to type to find them, listing those words as you go. Then, using the words you listed, 45 minutes of focused searching followed by a cuppa.

At the end of that hour you may not feel like you have made a huge dent in your overall journey of taking your idea to reality, but in that salami step, you completed a very necessary task, you nailed it. You can tick that step off. Feel good and work out what's the next one to tackle.

the salami steps way gives you reasons to celebrate each small achievement

Doing it the salami steps way gives you reasons to celebrate each small achievement. That celebration relights your passion and drives you forward. Instead of having days when you feel frustrated that you seemingly have not achieved much, you can tick off and celebrate each step.

We may look at others who are successful and think that it must have been easy for them, but it seldom is in reality. They may have made it look easy, but it never is the case that they had a business idea and it just happened without effort. The discipline of completing each individual task on your list is the key to success. So don't start setting up a spreadsheet for customer orders and then stop to call your designer, and return to your list to start something completely different. Before stopping one task to start another, ask 'Have I made a dent in this?' If you haven't, that snack, TV time or phone call can wait. It's about staying focused on your productivity for 60 minutes at a time.

You will need to make a lot of decisions on your journey, and here's how we can make that easier for you.

THE 60-SECOND DECISION

Having mastered the 60-Minute Task, we would now like to introduce you to our super fast way to make a decision. And of course it's easy to do, effective and has been devised to keep you moving forward quickly towards your goal of launching your business. It's our 60-second decision. Here's how it works: you run into a problem; instead of spending all night laying awake in bed thinking about it, write the problem down. Just a sentence will do. Now give yourself no more than 60 seconds to make the decision. Is it a yes or a no? Should the logo be round or square? Is the font Verdana or Arial? Make the decision and stick with it until either it stays forever or more insight comes in to your world and you can see clearly the benefits of changing it. But that changing of your mind must only be derived from gaining further insight, not on a whim. People who make decisions quickly and change them slowly tend to do much better in business and life in general. Film directors know that the finiteness of making a decision is critical to keeping a movie moving forward and all the cast and crew enthusiastic. If the director seems somewhat unsure of a decision and can't make their mind up, then the cast and the crew will quickly start to lose faith in the director's ability, and so a downward spiral begins that ends in a failed project. Good film directors make a quick and firm decision, right or wrong, they make it based on gut instinct which is built upon years of being around cameras, cast, crew and telling and hearing compelling stories. They take all that wisdom locked in their minds and make a quick decision based on the information they have to hand. If they are wrong, they re-shoot the scene. Not exactly the end of the world is it?

> people who make decisions quickly and change them slowly tend to do much better in business and life in general

Most decisions can be dealt with in a flash. David just phoned Ian with a small decision about spending money. We agreed it quickly, the call took less than 60 seconds. There wasn't any 'let's talk about that later' or 'I need to think about that' – the risk was low so we just pressed go. How often in organisations and bigger businesses do those kind of questions turn into big meetings or conference calls? If there's initial indecision, then there's the tendency to say 'we'd better ask Lisa' or 'do we need to check that with Head Office?' or 'let's wait to the management meeting and ask everyone what they think'. But instead of that, use your instinct and make an instant decision. We reckon that even those people that get lost in the process or meetings to make decisions; nine times out of 10 they end up going with the decision they first thought of.

If you don't embrace rapid decision making, you'll struggle to make a success of your idea. Sarah Beeny is the property expert, TV presenter and entrepreneur who juggles multiple projects, businesses as well as four young children (and a dog). There's only one way she can make this happen, by rapid decision making: She told us:

> *I like things to happen, and I like things to happen quickly. If you work in the corporate world it takes a tremendous long time to make things happen and that would frustrate me enormously. I'm used to making my own decisions. One phone call and I can make enormous decisions.*

All new businesses have to start out in the same place. At the beginning with nothing. As the journey begins so some of those will thrive as they complete each small salami slice and some businesses will stall as the founders try to take on the mammoth task in one big bite. Only a small percentage of business start-ups will make it to the first invoice. Those will be the ones that methodically work through the salami steps with great persistence and passion. Employing the 60-Minute Task and the 60-Second Decision will enable you to slice through your journey from idea to launch.

ZOOM THINKING

1 Go and buy a pack of Post-its and a marker pen. Clear your kitchen table and start mapping out your journey.

2 Sixty minutes to get this done. You'll be amazed at how much can be achieved.

3 Sixty seconds to make a decision. No excuses!

11

Telling your story

MAKING YOUR BUSINESS STAND OUT FROM THE CROWD

At the heart of every great business is its story. Your story is what people remember about your business and how people will describe your business to other people. People may care deeply about the benefits of an organic baby food product but people will remember the story behind it long after it has fed a hungry mouth.

The story of a mother frustrated when she couldn't find the right food for her newborn. So, as a response, she developed a product in her kitchen for mothers just like her. Other mothers will relate to her quest, they will feel an emotional connection with her and they will remember her story. So when faced with a choice in the supermarket, they may just choose the product that resonates with them as a mother. It's the story that's going to win it for you.

Think of your story as acting like a magnet. Sure, you may have a great website and a marketing campaign ready to roll out but your story is what will attract interest. Marketing can be impersonal especially if your business creates a product that is difficult for people to relate to; they may not care about the ability of your software to deliver data-driven solutions for engineering clients, but they might be interested in your story. Of how you quit your job as a stockbroker and retrained as a software engineer. Now that's a story that will make us prick up our ears, right?

When Will King launched his shaving product King of Shaves sceptics asked how could he succeed? How could be compete with the big established brands like Gillette? Will may not have been able to compete with the giants on their advertising budgets but he could compete on his story. His story tells of how 18 years ago razor burn led him to experiment with his girlfriend's bath oil in an attempt to overcome the problem. He eventually had a breakthrough and that led to an innovative new product. A product he was determined to share with the world. Normally, a person would heed the warning of others concerned that he was wasting his time going up against the big manufacturers with their huge budgets and to give up on the journey now. But Will King was on a quest, the little guy up against the big guys and people love that. They love a story of fighting against adversity, of achieving against all odds. Now the King of Shaves story is an important differentiator.

And now, 18 years later, there is a powerful new platform within Will's reach and within all our reach that enables us to amplify our story. King of Shaves may lack Gillette's billboard budget but Will lives and breathes his brand 24/7 telling his ongoing story online, using social media to reinforce his authenticity as a hero on a quest. Your coffee shop, your software business, whatever your business is, you can use social media to create a narrative.

So, how do you write your story? Every time we sit down to read a novel, watch a film or a play we are experiencing a new story. Yet it is said that nearly every single story ever told is derived from one of just seven plots. They are:

> it is said that nearly every single story ever told is derived from one of just seven plots

1   **The quest**: the story of a hero attempting to meet a difficult distant goal.

2   **Voyage and return**: like the quest only the hero will return (usually much wiser).

3   **Rebirth**: escaping from a dark spell.

4   **Tragedy**: does what it says on the tin, the downfall of someone who is usually powerful at the start.

5   **Overcoming the monster**: the hero must kill the dark evil entity.

6   **Rags to riches**: from zero to hero very quickly.

7   **Comedy**: any of the above only add lots of misunderstanding.

Stories are made up of three components. A beginning, where the story is set up. The middle, this part helps if it includes some tension or conflict, and an end with an outcome.

The plots of the quest, voyage and return, overcoming the monster and rags to riches all lend themselves to business starters.

Next you will need to find the emotional angle to your story. That's emotion, not facts. People are not emotionally turned on by statistics, so look for the human truth in your story and practise telling it. You may feel way out of your depth here. Think of your friends and family, who is the story teller? Who is the friend who gets asked to be best man? Who loves to tell jokes? Go to them and ask them to help add emotion to your story. Natural story tellers have a way of fitting the plot together in a compelling way and they usually relish at the opportunity to help.

look for the human truth in your story and practise telling it

So if you are struggling to define your own story try asking yourself these questions to see what kind of story you are. You only need to be able to answer one with a yes and you will be on the path to establishing your story.

→ **Did you solve a problem?** This is the quest or voyage and return plot. Your journey to solve the problem would have been filled with drama. Edison failed to invent the light bulb 10,000 times before he finally succeeded.

→ **Did you take a big risk?** Did you, like Jamie Oliver once did, use your family home as collateral to get your idea off the ground? Risking everything in a single-minded pursuit of your goal?

→ **Did you discover something new and are now sharing it with the world?** Whilst on a completely unrelated journey did you come across some interesting nugget that became your new business?

→ **Is a famous person involved?** Get them to talk about you, people tend to listen to famous people.

→ **Did you achieve success for an incredibly small amount of money or in a super fast time?** If your start-up went from idea to trading in 24 hours, like Dr Hue, the shopping by colour website, then you have a story. If you launched your business for less than a price of a bunch of flowers, then good for you too, now start telling people.

→ **Are any cute animals involved in your business?** People love pets, they make us very emotional so any positive way of involving your family pet in the story won't go amiss. You might be thinking what are we doing talking about pets? But journalists know the power of animal stories for selling newspapers. Seriously!

→ **Are you on a journey that your friends are curious about?** Starting a business takes a huge leap of faith. If your friends and family are interested in how you are progressing, hearing your ups and downs, then others will be too.

→ **Are people getting excited about your product or service?** If you have created something that is creating excitement amongst your customers, then they will become your story tellers. Evangelists are a powerful group and very valuable to you. Keep them close. Keep them informed. Keep them happy.

→ **Have you created something that is novel?** We love novelty but novelty alone tends to wear thin quite quickly. So ride the novelty wave but be ready with another angle or story for when the novelty fizzles out.

So once you can tell your story, you will want people to hear it: blog about your journey as an entrepreneur, how it's tough juggling a three-month old baby with a jewellery business. Tweet your successes, your

word of mouth marketing is by far the most powerful form of marketing that exists

challenges and how you overcome them. Update your status with thoughts and feelings about your new life. Make your website reflect your story. Talk to journalists about your story but most importantly tell customers your story and they will in turn tell others. That's called word of mouth marketing and is by far the most powerful form of marketing that exists. And better still, it's free.

It goes without saying that your story must be authentic, it's no good creating some out there tale that is simply not true, it's got to be real and come from your heart, be personal. It's got to connect with people and inspire them to take action. It's primary purpose is not to 'sell product' but to take your customers, those that discover you, on a journey. It is on that journey, it may last a sentence, it may be a page, it's on that journey that they feel emotion towards you and your offering.

Last year Ian went to visit a small manufacturing business in Essex that makes bolts for construction projects. Nothing too exiting so far. Excalibur Screwbolts is a small business run by the founder who invented the screwbolt, Charlie Bickford. Charlie's story is a classic tale of overcoming the monster, Charlie had a villain he needed to kill that came to light whilst he was running a plastering company. Charlie became frustrated with the shortcomings of conventional bolts and their lack of ability to stay in old walls. So faced with the problem he invented a bolt that can be screwed into any hard material. His first big job using his new bolt was to repair the roof of the riding school at Buckingham Palace. His bolt proved perfect for the job and 20 years later that royal connection came full circle when Excalibur Screwbolts won a Queen's Award for Enterprise, an award for industry bestowed by Her Majesty. Now this isn't a huge company with a chain of warehouses around the world, it's an unremarkable building on an unremarkable trading estate in Essex where the 75-year-old owner still answers the phone. Yet his invention serves an impressive range of engineering projects from the Olympic Stadium in Atlanta to the Gotthard Tunnel in Switzerland. And whilst like Will King and Gillette, Charlie can never beat the big construction giants with advertising budgets, his story is what gets his company talked about and what keeps their order books full. When site managers, project engineers and construction companies want to source some bolts, they may just elect to go to the bloke who invented the bolt that fixed the Queen's roof.

Your story is important. It's what will define you and your business. Your story will inspire your team, convey your passion to your audience and be the differentiator in a crowded marketplace. Understand your story, shape it, tell it and retell it.

ZOOM THINKING

1 Your story will differentiate you from the competition and make you memorable in the minds of your customers. So, craft a convincing but authentic story, based on personal experience and emotion rather than on dry facts and stats.

2 People love passion, so tell your story like you care about it passionately.

3 What's our story? Find out here:
   www.thezoomguys.com

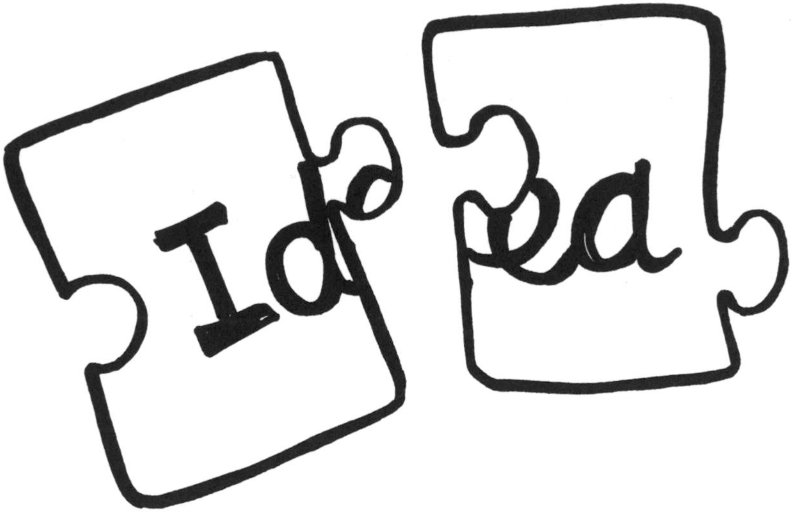
Id
ea

12

Think like a kid

WHY YOU SHOULD KEEP IT SIMPLE

The trouble with business today is that we over complicate things. We get so wrapped up in procedure, meetings and presentations that we lose sight of the simplicity of our ideas. We tend to dilute what was wonderful about an idea by adding layers of complexity such as jargon, strategies and difficult to understand explanations.

We put process and obstacles between thoughts and making those thoughts real. What comes out the other end is a great idea crushed by complexity born out of over thinking. What we really need is to think like a kid. To keep things simple. So stuff gets done.

And that's the problem. Remember when you were just a kid? Stories were simple, easy to recall and they made sense. Cowboys and Indians chased each other, whilst princesses waited for a prince on a white horse to arrive. Your imagination was free to manipulate any object to fit your story. A stick could be either a gun or a horse. A play tent could be a fortress or a fairytale castle. Everything was a game and your curiosity was in abundance. As a kid you were encouraged to stand out, be an individual and dream.

Then you went to school and the rules changed. You had to learn how to fit in, learn to recite formulas and stop dreaming. You had to sit at a desk for most of the day and your wild thoughts and actions were reserved for playtime. Basically the opposite of everything that was great about being a kid.

Then you started work and you provide a service in exchange for money. Now you're following process, protocol and orders. You try not to stand out too much so that you can fit in to the new company. You can't find a job code for dreaming so you curtail that behaviour. You take the simple things and wrap them in complex jargon and three letter acronyms, because everyone else is, and you want to fit in. Most organisations aren't flexible enough at letting people explore their creativity. We remember the story of the business where we first met, where Ian was a project manager and David a creative. David asked his boss if he could go and sit by a lake for a day to think up ideas for radio programmes. Guess what the response was? But if you thought like a child, you would want to have your best thoughts in a tent, your den at the bottom of the garden, a tree-house or sitting by a lake. Don't fool yourself in to thinking that you're going to come up with great ideas sitting in a boardroom. You have got to get out and play!

A friend showed us an email from a cleaning company that did some domestic cleaning once a week. The home owner had sent an email complaining that some of the cleaning jobs had not been carried out that week. The reply that came back from the cleaning company resembled something from a legal department of a pharmaceutical giant that was being sued for distributing killer drugs to babies in the Third World. But it was a small neighbourhood cleaning company! It actually referenced sub clauses in their terms and conditions and didn't offer a simple solution. The friend sent another email asking for the cleaning company to explain what the message actually meant. He received another full legal reply complete with unfathomable jargon. It took three exchanges for the friend to get a straight answer to the original complaint. A lot of wasted time for the business owner and a lesson in how not to treat customers. But the important lesson here is that simple, honest communication, the kind that a kid demands, would have been the most effective way to deal with the problem. And the sad point here is that the cleaning company is not alone in its pursuit of complicating everything. This kind of complexity wastes valuable time, frustrates people and is not logical. Those older than 30 may remember that American sitcom, *Diff'rent Strokes*, where the kid used to say, 'What'cha talkin' about Willis?'. Try saying that every time you're faced with jargon, process and procedure. Bring it back to kid-level; don't let others complicate it up.

bring it back to kid-level; don't let others complicate it up

So – it's time to bring back the simple.

Here's an example of a company thinking like a kid. You've probably seen the Flip camera. Ever so simple yet ever so effective. A minimum of buttons and controls. A modest zoom, a record, play and delete button. That's about it. When Flip released their camera the market was already saturated with video cameras. Each manufacturer trying to outdo each other with another feature. Anti-shake, special effects, 80 × digital zoom and a whole load more. So how could Flip enter this saturated market as an unknown, up against brand names with years of manufacturing history behind them? Flip thought like a kid and made it simple. So simple that anyone could use it. No external mic, no back light, anti-shake or any other gadget. Just shoot your video and then plug your camera into your laptop for upload. It doesn't even require a cable to connect to your computer. We love it. The designers could have easily added more functionality, more buttons, lots of features, but they didn't. It's such a simple idea and it has really caught on because of its simplicity.

So can we turn back the clock and think like a kid? Of course we can. It starts by questioning everything with that simple innocence that only a kid possesses. Ask questions of yourself and your business and wait until you discover the most simple logical explanation. Is all that text required to explain your story? Is it even a story? Or does it read like the instruction manual for a nuclear power plant? If so strip it back and imagine you are explaining the subject to a friend down the pub. Once you've mastered that, how would you explain it to a nine year old? Now at some point you may need to mock up an element of your business, a prototype perhaps. Why not build it from discarded household items and hold it all together with sticky tape. It may not win any awards, but you will be able to 'play' with your prototype on the kitchen table, making adjustments as you go until you have what you really want. And that play element is very important. By playing with problems, looking at them from different angles,

ask questions of yourself and your business and wait until you discover the most simple logical explanation

imagining they are something different but suffering the same condition, you can start to remove the blinkers that we have conditioned ourselves to wear. That liberation will give you a view of your product or service that is a unique perspective. An uncompromised slant on your business that brings to light fresh opportunity, previously hidden behind the exterior of sensible grown up thinking. So go on, get the crayons out and have some fun. Learn to play with problems to find the solution, ask professionals who are providing you a service 'why' something is the way it is, and keep asking why until you fully understand. And if it doesn't make sense to you, change it. Don't be afraid to hold your hand up during a meeting and ask what the acronym actually means, how the widget will benefit anyone and how stuff works?

Thinking like a kid will get you into places and spaces that will shine a spotlight on the bleeding obvious that is often hidden behind a curtain of adult complexity.

So is it time you looked at your world through some fresh eyes? Eyes that are not inhibited by the way others have deemed acceptable? Eyes that are playful and inquisitive? We spend far too much time as it is playing the part of adults. All grown up and sensible. Now give some thought and time to thinking like a kid.

we spend far too much time playing the part of adults

ZOOM THINKING

1 How can you apply thinking like a kid to your business?

2 Is your website just too complicated and your offering needing communicating in straightforward language?

3 Are you trying to add too many features or buttons to something that works perfectly well?

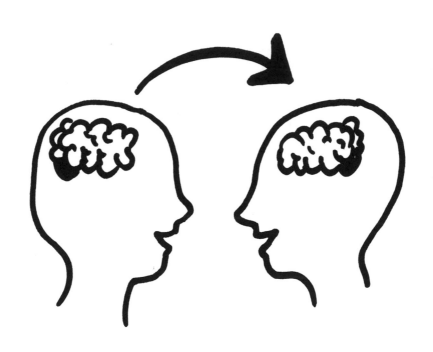

13

The power of collaboration

WHEN TWO MINDS ARE BETTER THAN ONE

Running a business is a bit like being a head chef, you have all these ingredients that you need to blend to create a dish that people will pay to eat. The chef needs to choreograph all the various elements that make up a fine meal.

That's task enough in itself without expecting the chef to grow the vegetables, tend the livestock and crush the grapes. So one thing is very clear: you won't be able to do everything yourself. You'll need to collaborate with others: from advisers and mentors to technical specialists and experts. The value in that collaboration – and the difference it will make to your end product – is powerful. As Richard Moross, founder of Moo.com said, 'None of us is as smart as all of us.'

One of the biggest challenges for an entrepreneur is balancing the desire to be self-sufficient with knowing when to bring in experts. Inevitably, you start out on your journey wanting to be lean so you do everything you possibly can yourself. But you soon learn it would be much more efficient to bring in an expert. Why invest all that time trying to master book-keeping when you could bring in a small business accountant to do that for you on a part-time basis? As Jeffrey Kalmikoff – one of the team behind Threadless – told us, you need to be clear where your strengths lie:

> *The common thread amongst entrepreneurs – whether they're adept at design, engineering, business development, leadership or any other specific area of concentration – is a solid network that fills in the gaps where your own expertise or skills don't cover. The best tool an entrepreneur can have is the ability to be honest with themselves about what they are and are not capable of.*

Collaboration comes in different shapes and sizes. Today with the growth in freelancers, home-workers and one person businesses, entrepreneurs have options to collaborate with serious talent via outsourcing. The benefit of outsourcing is that it keeps risks and overheads low, you only pay for the external help when you need it. Indeed, we heard one woman describe how she and her business partner had made a strategic decision to outsource everything from manufacturing to PR and answering the phone, all to freelance home-workers. They even outsourced warehousing meaning they did not need to take the risk on hiring space and personnel with all the headaches that brings. Instead they were liberated to drive the business forward and focus on the stuff they were good at.

Before you consider collaborating with someone you need to answer this question: are they the kind of person who can solve the kind of problems that you have? It may be that the problems you need solving have no known solution. In which case this question really is important. You are looking for someone who you believe can solve your problems, not someone who is good at reminding you that the problem needs fixing. There is a difference. One will roll up their sleeves and with entrepreneurial spirit will take ownership of the problem and will positively thrive in solving it. The other will lose interest and admit defeat too quickly. To distinguish between the two at the interview stage ask these questions. What groups or organisations do they belong to that relate to their field of work? The expert who cannot solve the problem but can call upon their peers to help is more valuable than the one who can't. How active are they in those groups? The one who is active will be adding more value to the group and will be more likely to get quick answers back from peers. Ask why they chose their profession. Some people work for money. Some work because they love what they do. The person to collaborate with is the one who loves what they do. They will not rest until they solve your problem.

the person to collaborate with is the one who loves what they do

You'll notice that there are two founders behind a lot of successful businesses. Two can be a magic number for staying focused and mixing the right mindset to make your idea happen. Look at the story behind *The Huffington Post*. 'HuffPo' may be well known because of its founder Arianna Huffington but her less well known partner Kenneth Lerer was the guy in the sidelines whose marketing and technology insight made the idea world famous and worthy of a $315 million offer from AOL. Arianna was the glitzy front-woman with access to celebrities and politicians; Kenneth focused on making it a business; first creating and then finally selling the brand. That kind of collaboration is dynamite.

collaboration could come from a meeting with a mentor, a lunch with a friend or a part-time adviser

The right kind of collaboration can provide immense value to your business idea. Some feedback you could have never anticipated, a really insightful and fresh perspective on your changing model or how you segment your products. Never underestimate that kind of value. Of course, you don't need to have a full-time collaboration to benefit from that input; it could come from a meeting with a mentor, a lunch with a friend or a part-time adviser. And if you can't afford advisers there are free online tools to help give you feedback on your idea.

Collaboration is going to be the way you will make your idea happen. So when do you turn a one-off collaboration in to a business partnership? Dave Stewart is known globally for being one half of the Eurythmics. Today he has taken his creative talent and turned it into a business, Weapons of Mass Entertainment, creating ideas that are genre and platform neutral. Dave told us about how he took ideas to prototype and then finds partners to make that happen:

> *Years ago, I used to have ideas and it used to do my head in, because I was trying to make them work by myself. But as I got older I realised, 'no, I'm an ideas person', I can take an idea through to prototype.*

If it's a TV series, Dave's company will shoot a little bit, give it a great title that would grab somebody's attention, and write a draft of how the series would be. But he doesn't try and make that series himself, he finds a production company that makes TV shows in that genre. Then he shares ownership in that idea to get it made; whilst he recognises that means he has to relinquish control it enables him to make the ideas happen:

I'd rather have 10% of something that took off than 100% of something that's still on the table. When you've got a whole ideas factory, then you've got 10% of 50 different things. They can all be happening at once, but we're not worrying about that because we're not the ones making them.

If you're going to collaborate, you need to open your mind to different ideas and different ways of doing things. That might be difficult for you if you're used to keeping control of your idea and you have very fixed views of how you want to run your business. But you've got to be a good listener and accept that you may not always have the right answer: someone else might.

Collaboration is not just necessary to make your idea happen, you need to collaborate or mix with other people and businesses for support and inspiration. California's Silicon Valley is famous for the right environment for incubating tech start-ups and so Palo Alto is where people go to develop tech ideas. When Ian visited Printer's Inc. Cafe in Palo Alto he noted how he was surrounded by laptop entrepreneurs, ideas that started out with a mint tea or espresso. That cluster of like-minded souls provided the catalyst for action. Now most cities have created their own tech districts, alive with people passionate about making their business work. In London, the roundabout at the junction of City Road and Old Street has been dubbed Silicon Roundabout, where tech companies have been developing together for four or five years. TechHub was founded in the area to help foster the local community. David Caldwell, a TechHub resident, was interviewd by the FT's digital correspondent, Tim Bradshaw:

you've got to be a good listener and accept that you may not always have the right answer: someone else might

13 THE POWER OF COLLABORATION

Having people around you who are also venturing their life savings on pursuing a dream is very important positive reinforcement. It also provides a resource to bounce ideas around and get feedback.
(Source: FT.com)

We spoke to TechHub's founder, Elizabeth Varley, who told us how important it is for developing businesses to get advice from similar companies a few months ahead of them: 'Sure, it's great to learn from experts but to learn from similar businesses six months or nine months in; that's really valuable'. Elizabeth believes sharing knowledge helps entrepreneurs solve their problems faster. It also creates an environment of like-minded souls which makes progress much easier. After all, it's difficult when people around you are telling you not to take risks; in an environment like TechHub everybody's taking risks. She told us that what tech entrepreneurs really needed was 'power, really good wifi, coffee and other great people'.

So take a look around where you live and seek out those gatherings where collaboration opportunity exists. Find people doing similar start-ups to yours, or even just start-ups and network with them. Your idea may be unique but your business problems are probably more similar to others than you can imagine.

ZOOM THINKING

1   Get used to looking for opportunities to collaborate with other people.

2   Be willing to help others, because you never know where that might lead.

3   What kind of space or cluster might help your business? Do you need to hang out in a co-working space, join a networking club?

ZOOM IN ON... RICHARD MOROSS
'Listen to advice'

Twitter: @richardmoross
Web: moo.com

Even though we live in a digital world, most people starting out need business cards. Moo.com has revolutionised the printing industry by applying web 2.0 principles and professional design principles, allowing customers to upload their own designs and create great business cards cheaply. With a simple mission 'great design for everyone', Moo now prints millions of cards a month and has hundreds of thousands of customers in over 180 countries.

Richard Moross is founder and CEO of Moo.com. He came up with the idea when he was 25, working for a design company. He was trying to think of a mass-market consumer product. Whilst business cards had been around so long they were essentially still an 'analogue' product, Richard felt that there was potential for a consumer-facing, web-based application. So Richard set out to create a new business-card product for consumers but also inextricably linked to the web.

Richard's tips for faster, easier ways to make your business idea happen:

1 If you're looking for investment, remember that investors look for two things, the kernel of a great idea and the right person to carry it through.

2 The biggest and hardest lesson was listening to other people's advice. If you surround yourself with really brilliant people who are willing to give their advice – listen to it.

3 You have to find the tastemakers and make your product so compelling and user friendly that people will become your brand evangelists and shout about it.

4 Be different. Moo are completely different to an offline printer shop that tends to be faceless. Moo say 'hello' – no one else does that in printing.

Video interview with Richard at **thezoomguys.com**.

13 THE POWER OF COLLABORATION

Magic Umbrella

HOW TO DEAL WITH CHALLENGES

There aren't many certainties in this unpredictable world of business. The truth is that no one knows what's around the corner. Sometimes it's a pleasant surprise, sometimes it's not. So what if your business hits an unforeseen obstacle? Customers do not love your idea, your website needs a redesign or your supplier disappears – how will you manage that challenge?

In an uncertain world, one thing is certain – you're going to get rained on at some point and when it starts to rain you'll need an umbrella. We've created a Magic Umbrella to help you and your idea stay dry, confident, optimistic and able to keep moving forward. To help us create the Magic Umbrella we've tapped into the fundamentals of how our minds work.

We know we should be optimistic if we want to be successful – that makes sense but how can we tune up our minds so that an optimistic outlook prevails? That's the holy grail, right? Well, consider this chapter as 'the science bit' – by understanding how your mind works and how you can stay optimistic – you can open your Magic Umbrella and be protected against that rainy day.

So you might be reading this in a coffee shop, on a train or perhaps in bed late at night. You're feeling OK. So what would happen if, say, a polar bear entered your train carriage right now? WTF!? What would you do? In your brain, many things would be happening simultaneously and without you consciously thinking about it. Your subconscious mind would first check in what we call your precedent library, the part of your mind where all previous memories are stored, and fairly quickly the instruction would come back for you to sweat to cool your muscles, increase heartbeat to get the blood pumping and run like the wind!

You wouldn't stop to question the sudden production of sweat, increased heartbeat or need to run away. It would just happen. No ifs, no buts. You wouldn't look at the polar bear and wonder if it has already had a large meal today and therefore isn't hungry. You wouldn't admire its fine fur and pet it. You wouldn't confer with your fellow commuters on the subject. You'd take off at speed and only once you had made a significant gap between you and the threat would you be able to start thinking for yourself again.

Everything up until that point is a pre-programmed reaction, nature's way of keeping the species alive.

All this takes place in the primitive part of our mind, the survival part, the subconscious part and that primitive mind dates back to the dawn of civilisation.

If our primitive mind thinks, for one reason or another that our life is in some kind of crisis or emergency, like a polar bear suddenly appearing, then it will move in to overcome that dangerous situation. When the primitive mind moves in to help, it moves in with one of three patterns: depression, anxiety and anger or a combination of all three. These are all primitive opt-out clauses. The one we will focus on here is anxiety as it is the most prevalent for business. Many things are going to test you both emotionally and mentally as you embark on your new venture, trying to turn your business idea into reality. Problems will arise when you least expect them, people will let you down and the unavoidable delay is going to happen. These kinds of unexpected issues will create anxiety, so the better you are at dealing with it, the better it is for you and your business. You need to stay in rational control during times that move you toward irrational instability. Let's face it, an actual polar bear isn't about to tear you to shreds. But, being let down, making a mistake, losing a deal may just feel like you've been chomped by that bear.

We will now outline the direct relationship between anxiety going up and our intellectual control simultaneously going down.

When our anxiety goes up we lose intellectual control. You can see that when we run into a polar bear. Our anxiety goes up, we lose intellectual control and our primitive mind steps in and takes over, to save us from the threat. It's the same in life. When our anxiety goes up in life, then we lose intellectual control because the emotional mind steps in and takes over. It's nature's way of protecting us from danger. Even

when the primitive mind moves in to help, it moves in with one of three patterns

though your business problem isn't life-threatening, your emotional mind will still step in. It only needs to THINK you are in some kind of danger and it will react. Also it's a negative mind; because it is there for our self-preservation, it will always encourage us to see things from the worst possible scenario. It's very vigilant, not wanting to miss anything that could be seen as a threat. It's also an obsessive mind, checking again and again that you are not in any danger. Most of all though, because our emotional mind is not our intellect, it can't be innovative. It always has to refer back to previous patterns of behaviour. Negative thoughts are always converted into anxiety.

It's also interesting to note that our primitive mind can't tell the difference between what we imagine happening, and what is actuality happening. So when we imagine something bad happening, to our primitive mind it is exactly the same as it happening. That is a thought worth considering, you can bring about anxiety just by imagining something negative happening. Let me give you an example – Dan works in an office, he doesn't speak to his boss that often and one morning the boss marches through the office and says 'Dan, I want to see you in the boardroom right now'.

What happens to Dan? His primitive emotional mind negatively forecasts that he must be in some kind of trouble – no facts to prove this is the case at this point, just what Dan is imagining in his own mind. Then he starts to panic a little… Was it the invoice he sent out yesterday, did he make a mistake with the costs? Was it the email he sent to a client explaining that the project was running late, had they complained? Now, as his anxiety levels creep up, Dan may well start to sweat, his hands feel clammy, he has a hot flush. These are real physical reactions to something Dan is only imagining. None of his thoughts is actually backed up by any evidence at this point; it's not real; it is all in his mind.

when we imagine something bad happening, to our primitive mind it is exactly the same as it happening

ZOOM! THE FASTER WAY TO MAKE YOUR BUSINESS IDEA HAPPEN

Dan may even begin to feel physically sick as the negative forecasting by his primitive emotional mind kicks up a gear. Anxious, feeling nauseous and fearing for his livelihood, Dan enters the boardroom and is told to sit down. 'Dan!', booms the voice of the boss. 'You've worked here for a while, you've got to know the people here, I want to know, what do you think of James in accounts, should we promote him?'

Only now, at the realisation that the negative forecasting was incorrect does Dan's heart rate begin to slow back to normal. Phew, you can relax…

In some way, we have all been in that position. Had those very same emotional feelings. Negative forecasting leading to a physical reaction. Just by imagining something, just by thinking it, we have a physical reaction. All because our primitive mind cannot tell the difference between what we imagine in our minds and what is real.

just by imagining something, just by thinking it, we have a physical reaction

That's one way to create anxiety, by negatively forecasting the future, like Dan. The other is to negatively retrospect. To look back at your past, five minutes ago or five years ago, you recall moments where you wish you had done things differently. Again, the primitive mind cannot tell the difference between what you imagine and what is happening to you right now. Negatively forecasting and retrospective negativity both lead to anxiety. Anxiety moves you from the rational mindset to an irrational mindset.

So let us create the Magic Umbrella to help get you through those unwanted adrenaline rushes that we will all suffer from at some point.

It is called the Magic Umbrella because an umbrella protects you from the rain and keeps you dry. This umbrella, being magic, means it will always be with you ready for use. And being an umbrella it will keep you sheltered from the shower.

Now you have an understanding of how your mind works, why we react and behave the way we do in certain situations, you are in the unique position of being able to stop a shower before it turns into a torrential downpour. Recognising that your anxiety levels are about to climb means you can intercept the negative forecasting and go some way to returning yourself to your most productive state of mind, the rational mindset. That's the good news: you can actually do something about anxiety. You have the power to take control of your own mind in these situations.

So whether the challenge comes from family, friends, supplier, customer, whenever the rain starts you can follow this simple set of steps:

1   When trouble strikes, even imaginary trouble, in your mind visualise yourself putting your umbrella up. Your umbrella that is always with you and is large enough to fully protect you from any downpour. It goes up with ease and locks into position with a positive click. It is made of quality materials and won't fail you. Ever. Believe it!

2   Your umbrella going up is a signal that you must remove yourself from a negative situation as quickly as possible. Making decisions for your business whilst you are not in your intellectual mind, that is, where you are over emotional or angry about the delay of a website or feeling let down by your partner, will only be detrimental to your mental state and achieving your goals.

3   You now need to park the problem. Remember the primitive mind is a negative mind, it will make the situation as terrible as it can as it thinks your life is in danger. Also it is an obsessive mind, so it will keep looping the problem until it has gone. If the problem cannot be solved immediately, then quickly write the problem down, we call this 'parking the problem'. By writing it down you have carried out an action related to the problem, you have not solved it but you have duly noted it. It is parked, it's in a box.

4   Now you need to distract your primitive mind from the problem and the best way to achieve this is by physical action. Exercise is the fastest way to create serotonin which is basically the happy drug. When we produce a constant flow of serotonin in the brain we are nice happy coping people. So your Magic Umbrella now has one role to perform. It needs to protect you whilst you make your way as quickly as possible to a 15 minute work out that will get the heart racing. A run around the block, pull-ups, weights, whatever it takes to get the pulse raised. Even a walk around the block. A cigarette or a double Jack Daniel's does not create serotonin. It will not work to lower your stress or anxiety, it may do for a fraction of time but it has been proven that the anxiety comes back very quickly and at a higher level. Eating is not an option nor is watching TV. Walking or exercise or even dancing around your front room is an option. You can tell your primitive mind that the Magic Umbrella is up so all is OK. Remember, the primitive mind can't tell the difference between what is real and what we imagine.

5   As soon as you are working out, creating serotonin, you need to force yourself to focus on solutions and not the problem. If you focus your attention on the problem, then the problem will appear bigger and move towards you. If you focus your attention on the solution, then the solution will appear bigger and move towards you.

6   You will need a reservoir of additional calm about you to be able to easily deal with unexpected problems that arise. So take advantage of times when you can relax, clear your mind of all thoughts and visualise yourself in a calm place, feeling relaxed and at ease.

Problems will come and problems will go. How you deal with them is how you will be measured. Practise

putting up your Magic Umbrella, informing your
subconscious mind that you have parked the problem
and creating serotonin as quickly as possible.

ZOOM THINKING

1   When trouble strikes, put that umbrella up.

2   Now the umbrella is up, you can park your
problem.

3   Go for that run around the block and start
making serotonin.

4   Get calm, get focused on solutions.

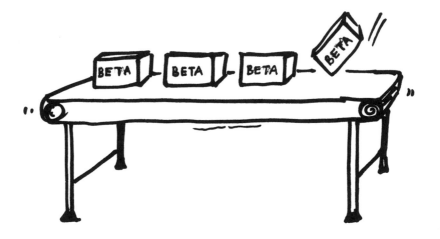

Launch in beta

WHAT YOU CAN LEARN FROM A SOFTWARE COMPANY

If you insist on tinkering with your product until you consider it perfect, then your business will probably never launch. The story of start-ups not reaching take-off because they ran out of cash or energy perfecting their offering is a sad but common one. So instead you need to think like a software company and launch your product or service when it's still in development.

Of course, your product or service must be fit for purpose, It needs to work, but it does not need to be perfect. Launching early means you can get feedback from customers and upgrade your offering as you go. Not only does this mean you can make your business idea happen rapidly, it also means you don't need to worry about whether your research about what the customer wants is 100% correct; instead you get real-life paying customers to give you feedback on user experience and service as you go.

Of course, there is a balance between launching in beta and launching unfit for purpose. To qualify as beta, your product or service must fulfil on its basic promise: it's got to work. If you have made a piece of software that alerts you when you overspend on your credit card, then it must at least do that. It may have issues when you load five or more credit cards through the software. It may have other little quirks that unfold as more people use it, but basically it must deliver on the promise.

Nowhere is this launch-in-beta approach more active than with mobile app developers. They acknowledge that the apps they're launching will require upgrades as soon as customers tell them what they like, and they discover what works and what doesn't. As customers we understand that's how the app market works, we'll still pay for an app, and benefit from upgrades as we require more functionality.

App developers have learnt that speed to market is crucial, in a world full of developers sitting in their spare rooms thinking up app ideas, the one who launches fastest wins. You've got to get it out there first, to land-grab, to target your niche, to evangelise your idea. Better to have an imperfect iteration of your idea out there then a perfect idea that never gets launched. We've been fans of the London Tube Exits app on our iPhones, put in your start tube station and your destination and it will tell you what tube carriage to

better to have an imperfect iteration of your idea out there then a perfect idea that never gets launched get in so you're by the exit when you get off. OK so it's not going to change the world but it's saved valuable seconds for Ian when he's been dashing home to read his kids that bedtime story. There was no data from the tube people to get this app working, the guy who created it had to sweat a lot, visiting stations, noting down positions of exits. So, some things might have been wrong. But that was OK. It was still a great idea. Sometimes it said try a middle carriage, rather than try the third carriage from the front. But with user feedback and more work, upgrades improved the experience. But no one slammed down their iPhones in disgust if something was wrong, most people knew it had been designed by a guy with modest resources, they'd only invested 79 pence. They loved the idea, and it mostly worked; certainly enough for word of mouth to spread amongst the London tweeters and bloggers to get it known. It delivered on its promise. So it wasn't perfect at launch but there was enough there to benefit the user, the creator spotted an opportunity and what's more he got there first. He won.

Venture captalist and entrepreneur Guy Kawasaki told us that the first step to building a business is not to boot Excel or PowerPoint or Word; it's to prototype:

If you're going to go into the cookie business, step one is not to plan out five years of how many chocolate chip cookies you're going to sell; step one is to make a batch of cookies and see if people beyond your family will pay for it! Step one in the technology business is not to write out a PowerPoint presentation; it's to get a website that's working or a piece of software that's demo-able. If you do all that and you get to market quick enough, you may never have to do a spreadsheet or a PowerPoint!

Launching in beta allows for experimentation, a critical part of taking your idea to market. Tom Peters emailed us from his holiday in New Zealand with his

Launching in beta allows for experimentation

take on the importance of prototyping, reminding us the importance of having something to shoot at if you want to move forward, quoting Ross Perot's motto of 'Ready. Fire. Aim'. Tom added, 'In 2010 in my speeches I claim (and mean it) that I've only learned one thing in 40 years' of business: "He who tries the most stuff the fastest wins".'

But there's another benefit to launching quick and often: it helps your commitment. On a psychological level, a business owner or project team thinks differently once a project is up and running. It ceases to be hypothetical and starts to feel very real. It's not stuck in the ghetto of a spreadsheet anymore, it's happening, it's launched, it's live. Giving yourself a more urgent – and real – deadline really focuses your talents. Because it's not a dress rehearsal anymore, it's out on stage in front of the audience. There is huge pressure, but that pressure can yield highly increased results. If you say you're going to debut your product at Spitalfields Market on the first Sunday in December and you've booked the stall, you have to deliver. The same with a shop opening or website launch. In the Aaron Sorkin drama about the fictional, Friday-night TV show, *Studio 60 On The Sunset Strip*, there is a scene where the two new junior writers just aren't coming up with good enough material to get a sketch on air. The senior writer knew why they weren't succeeding; because they believed their scripts would end up on the writing room floor. The fact that their material getting to air was so slim meant they didn't try hard enough: their efforts, were academic. But imagine how that would change if they knew that – good or bad – their writing would end up on air? The senior writer said to the exec producer:

There's no pressure. They don't have to do anything. They know that. They're trying but they know they are not getting anything on the air.

Lesson one: they've got to live or die on Friday night. They've got to feel like success in a three-minute sketch is the same thing as love and they've got to fear failure...

It's the same with your business idea, if you are just playing around with your product or service because you know it's not going to get launched yet, switch the focus. Say you're going to launch it. Set a date, start the countdown clock on your holding page, commit – near perfect or perfect, and you will be surprised at just how good your results are.

Launching in beta also makes your business more manageable, because you can launch small and scale up when your customers are there. Instead of worrying about setting up a production line operation to produce 1,000 units why not focus on producing 50 or 100 units first? Launching a product in different versions and upgrading as you go helps you build relationships with customers beyond a single transaction to multiple transactions. If you are able to upgrade your products offering more often to your customers you can keep them interested.

So what if you don't produce mobile apps or you're not a web-based business, how does 'launch in beta' apply to you? If you're a florist, embracing 'launch in beta' might mean you open your shop with a small choice of flowers rather than a big one; you might experiment with prices before setting your ratecard; see whether there is demand for gift cards as well as flowers; experiment on promotions and opening times. It's better for your business – and for your neighbourhood – to have an operational florist, even if the idea is still in development when you first open the doors to customers. You can always reinvent and improve your offering once the shop is up and running. Nothing is set in stone.

most companies launch too late rather than too early

Guy Kawasaki* told us that most companies launch too late rather than too early and that you'll never know what is great until you get your product into the hands of real life customers:

I'm not saying you should ship a piece of crap, you should ship something great but if you try to ship something great that is perfect, you're going to take too long. You'll learn more about your product in the first week after shipping than 52 weeks thinking about and studying and doing focus groups. Your research is shipping, that's what market research is: Ship!

ZOOM THINKING

1 Feel the pressure of going live.

2 Launch as fast as you can, better to have a near-perfect idea launch than you never launch your perfect idea.

3 Use social media to listen to customers – get feedback, monitor, evaluate and tweak accordingly.

---

*Video interview with Guy at **thezoomguys.com**.

ZOOM IN ON... ELIZABETH VARLEY
'Getting better, faster'

Twitter: @evarley
Web: techhub.com

Co-working spaces don't just offer cheaper alternatives to renting offices; they also nurture collaboration. TechHub is the London co-working space for technology entrepreneurs that provides desk space and the opportunity to share ideas. Elizabeth Varley and Mike Butcher saw there was no focal point for the European/UK tech start-up scene, so they founded TechHub, getting support from Pearson and Google to keep costs down for the resident companies.

TechHub's mantra is to help tech start-ups to get better, faster and Elizabeth believes that by learning from similar businesses six months or nine months ahead of you is really valuable. Sharing that kind of knowledge helps entrepreneurs solve their problems quicker.

Elizabeth's tips for faster, easier ways to make your business idea happen:

1   Learn and recognise when you can't do everything yourself. You've got to learn when it's better to hire someone else to do something.

2   If someone else launches before you, learn from the competition. Don't make the mistakes as the first one to market.

3   Embrace and learn from failure. It's good to say: 'This isn't working. It needs to change.'

4   People get bogged down by plans, they never actually start it. Planning feels like you're doing something when you're not; you've got to put something out there, try something.

16

Your Launch Day

HELL YEAH!

There comes a point in your journey when your idea is speeding towards launch and there's no stopping it. You've been learning on the go, winging it at times, made some good decisions and some bad ones too. What you thought would look great in green turned out to be much better in red; you've heard more conflicting advice than you previously believed possible and you have dealt with the ups and the downs on your journey to launch.

Welcome to the beginning of your new business and oh, by the way, CONGRATULATIONS! You made it happen.

So this is the day that you have been aiming for since you first said, 'I want to start my own business.'

Your idea has finally transformed into a life of its own. It still needs you to hold it together, to nurture and to guide it. Your hard work isn't over yet, but now you should press the pause button, look back for a moment at all the amazing things that have happened because you made that decision to start. At any one time all over the world people are coming up with ideas for new products and businesses. Some are doing something about their idea; others not. So the fact that you made it to launch is a reason to pat yourself on the back.

So no more, 'when I launch', no more 'what if?' – it's real now. You've done it. Inevitably, you've been on a roller-coaster ride. Starting from that moment of inspiration you had about going into business, followed by the ups and downs as you steered your idea along, those days where you were convinced that this would never work for one reason or another. All of those emotions led to you being at this day, Launch Day. And now it is real. You've done it. Whatever your successes from now on may look like, the fact that you reached Launch Day is an indicator of success: many people never make it here so well done. It's time to yell at the top of your voice, 'Hell yeah!'.

One thing you can be sure of is that Launch Day will be both exciting and frightening in equal measures. Frightening because all the hard work, the sweat and the tears that you have gone through to take your idea from a thought in your mind to a real thing will now be out in the world, raw, for all to judge. You can see why so many people fail to actually launch the business now, can't you? Just that fear of letting outsiders judge what you have created is enough to bring the strongest out in a cold sweat. But here you are, up and running. You distinguished yourself from the others by persevering and making your idea happen.

And let's not forget the excitement. As the anticipation built, friends and family wishing you luck, even the doubters will be rooting for you as your new chapter comes closer. That moment is surely something to pause, reflect and then mark in some way. It's important that you acknowledge these events; this moment will form the DNA that will be your business story. In years to come these moments will be recalled with fondness, like when viewing a gracefully faded family photo. This is priceless material that reinforces your business culture, the meaning and the passion of your business.

> acknowledge these events; this moment will form the DNA that will be your business story

The goal you set at the start of your journey may have been to see your product on the shelf in a shop, win your first customer or launch your website. Entrepreneur Chris White, who has launched a portfolio of creative businesses including product development company, Bluw, explained to us the thrill of seeing his first customer buy one of their products:

> *I remember going to Superdrug with my business partner Charlie. We watched this woman come along and pick up this small gadget for the bathroom (made by Bluw). We followed her all the way to the till and she bought it. Charlie and I went 'Yes' – it was so brilliant. It was like scoring a goal at Wembley, it was such a thrill.*

With the adrenalin release of achieving your goal comes something new. Your product is out there, it's out of your hands now, it's in the hands of your customers. So be prepared for some surprises – hopefully pleasant ones – as your customers give you feedback on your idea. We just received some fridge magnets from new business start-up StickyGram, a service that turns your Instagram photographs from your mobile phone into fridge magnets. So having got our magnets, we then got asked for our feedback. What could be done to improve them, what should the price be? That kind of user feedback is invaluable for Stickygram creator, Kejia Zhu, as he develops his idea. So with the celebration of that launch comes something else: now it's out of your control, your customers will decide whether this is going to be a hit or a miss. Will they love it so much they'll get tweeting and blogging and telling their friends. Or will it go down as just another idea that didn't quite hit the spot?

Of course, like many things we look forward to, 'Launch Day' can be amazing or it can be an anticlimax. We want yours to be amazing. That way you will feel energised in a positive way and ready for the next stage of your journey. Topping up with that positive energy is important and feeling the success of making your business happen will provide you with that energy. If only you could bottle that stuff, it would be worth a fortune. So you don't want to let this moment slip by without preparing for it or it will be a bit like a New Year's Eve where you get all excited in anticipation but it ends up a huge let down. You need to mark that moment when you pull the lever, take your website live, open your shop doors, when the money comes in, when you've signed up your first customer or shipped your first product. Mark the occasion with a fitting celebration.

So you need to think about your Launch Day well in advance, you don't want to be ringing everyone who deserves to celebrate it with you after the event, you want them present *for* the event. Who should you invite? Your business may be very small, conceived by you, built by you and launched by you. If this is the case then consider your friends and family. Get them together, thank them for their support, open a bottle of something and mark the occasion. Share with them the stories and take time to listen, even the most critical of relatives and

think about your Launch Day well in advance, you don't want to be ringing everyone who deserves to celebrate it with you after the event friends will find it in their heart to give you some extra, and probably much needed, support today. Those present will then know what story to tell others and so your business is getting some highly valuable word of mouth marketing. If your business is a large operation that required support staff, then you really must get everyone together and invite both online and local press, they love a success story. It's time to say thank you to those who have in any small way at all been involved in the progression of your project. These people have provided the emotional fuel that has kept you going; they have delivered the intelligence, expertise and knowledge that you required to get your business up and running. Others have quietly kept you sane, believed in you when self doubt reared its head and given you a much needed smile when only bad news seemed to fill the air. Some of these people will be a big part of your next chapter and showing appreciation is a more powerful way of thanking them than the small amounts of money you've spent with them so far. All we ever want as people is to be acknowledged and appreciated for what we have done, and this is the perfect opportunity for you to do it. Your business, after all, will still need more energy tomorrow morning and having thanked everyone involved properly you should feel OK about asking for further assistance.

So, parties, champagne and patting each other on the back is all very well, but what's the point, where does all this celebration lead? How will it help your business move forward faster?

Well, a gathering is a great occasion for those that have been involved so far to meet each other. Your web designer probably hasn't met your supplier and neither has she met your accountant. So it's a great chance for everyone to network. And as for the helpers, supporters and freelancers that are based outside your country? Send them a bottle of something sparkling and Skype them in. It may be three in the morning where they are but they will join for a few minutes. You will be pleasantly bringing people who care about what you are doing together in one place will get them talking, problem solving

surprised as you get all these people together just how quickly the focus of the conversation turns to your business. The web lady chatting to the accounts guy discovers a simple more effective way of sharing important financial data. The drop shipping company meets the warehouse manager and realise that they have an outreach branch closer to the warehouse, cutting down on unnecessary transportation costs. You get the idea, bringing people who care about what you are doing together in one place will get them talking, problem solving and thinking of better ways of more effectively achieving your business goals.

As well as all the brain power gathered in one room thinking about and sharing ideas about your business, you will also have a chance to make a speech. That speech is the opportunity for you to reiterate your vision. When you say it out loud, write it down, share it with others that's the way you go about making something real. It's out of the box, it has a momentum of its own and you may be surprised how that articulation will drive your business forward. You may decide to deliver a speech to thank everyone, talk about the journey so far and close with your vision for the next chapter of your business. Publicly speaking about that next chapter will plant the seed with all those present as to what your intentions are. It becomes real. Suddenly the people who understand your business, who are all gathered in the same room, who have ideas on how things can be done better will know what your intentions are. They will talk about them over drinks and share ideas on how to most effectively achieve your vision. So don't get drunk, it's time to stay sober so you can soak up those conversations and learn.

Something else happens when you go live. The day you open your shop, launch your website, start trading something happens… you walk taller.

You are bursting with confidence that you defied the naysayers, you proved all those people wrong who shook their heads and said you should have stuck with your old job. You did it. That confidence is powerful, the fact that your dreams and aspirations have been validated will fuel your self-belief and help you on the next stage of your business journey. It will spur you on and equip you for what lies ahead.

But like any opening night or debut, the emotions include highs and lows. You're in uncharted territory now, the genie is out of the lamp, the idea is now in the real world and you have less control over your idea. Your customers will dictate whether it is a success or not.

With the serotonin racing around your mind, the adrenalin pumping around your body you should certainly be feeling on top of the world. This is a time where some might become complacent and just sit back; stop using all the tools that got them this far to get them even further. But right now, with the knowledge of what you are capable of doing, now is the time to seize this opportunity of great feeling and set about achieving your new goals. Chart that new course. Realise the next steps. If you need some help, maybe it is time to read Chapter 4 'Set a goal' one more time.

ZOOM THINKING

1 Celebrate. Mark the moment with whatever currency of celebration is appropriate. Pop open the champage; order the Nando's chicken, whatever.

2 Press 'Pause'. Stand back, reflect, pat yourself on the back, see how that moment matched your expectations, your goals, your visualisations.

3 Refuel your inspiration tank. Take a night away in a hotel, a run in the park, an afternoon at an art gallery – whatever it takes – to get inspired and to have the energy to deal with whatever is next (we'll talk more about this in Chapter 17).

Create a dashboard

ADJUSTING YOUR BUSINESS FOR SUCCESS

Your business is trading and people are buying your product or service. That's a great feeling. So far your new business may have required late nights, difficult decisions and far too many espressos. But you are up and running, what you imagined in your mind all those weeks ago is now real.

So now is the time to ask some important questions to establish if what you dreamed of is what you are actually doing. It's time to create your very own dashboard so you can gauge where you are. Just like the dials on a car dashboard inform you how your engine is performing and warns you if you are about to run out of fuel, this one will tell you what is going on in the business. This dashboard will alert you to what is going well and warn you if something is about to fail.

Creating your own dashboard is essential because whilst you might have access to the constituent elements, it's completely different when you look at it all together. And having that overview is what the dashboard gives you. Your sales figures might be telling you business is good and you're making good money this month, but what's the point of it all if you know deep down you are not satisfied or stimulated by what you're doing because you find it so soul-destroying? You can't look at one piece of information in isolation; you have to look at it all together. So the dashboard is powerful because what it does is recognise there is more than one metric, more than one measurable. It then enables you to get a clear view on your important metrics. Over time your business dashboard will factor many different measurable components including factors such as personal satisfaction, inspiration and happiness. Alongside all the obvious commercial indicators such as finance and customer satisfaction. This will help you establish if you are in danger of being profitable and unfulfilled or unprofitable yet fulfilled. The dashboard will give you an indication so you know what action to take, what tweaks to make so both the journey and your business are viable on every level. Being in control and informed, being able to see clearly how things are going will better inform you to make clear decisions. Decisions that are so often in business made only on impulse can now be spotted and acted upon with confidence.

So how do you make a dashboard? Firstly, you will need to list up all the things about your business that are important to you. This will require adding to your original reason for launching a business. Then you quite simply score everything out of 1 to 10, 1 being fatal and in need of immediate attention, and a score of 10 being excellent and no action required.

Don't spend too long thinking about the answers, you know if you are waking up every morning excited at the prospect of working in your own company that you are probably an 8 to 9 on the emotional satisfaction dial, so score it as that. On the other hand, if you pull the duvet over your head, then you may be a 3 or 4 and need to work on that area so mark it on the dial as that. Be truthful, sometimes the truth is not pretty, but better to deal with a not very attractive problem today then wait for it to turn into a hideous one tomorrow.

The good news is that however bad things may seem right now, things can be changed. That's why the dashboard is there, to show you what needs changing quickly. That way you can change the company to fit you before it changes you to fit it. It's by addressing the problems right now, before they take a hold and destroy what you have created so far, that you will stay in control.

Here are some ideas for dials you may want to create:

→ Emotional status (Happy to Sad)

→ Personal satisfaction (Satisfied to Dissatisfied)

→ Financial achievement

→ Health

→ Income

→ Spending

decisions that are so often in business made only on impulse can now be spotted and acted upon with confidence

→ Customer satisfaction

→ Profitability

→ Family time

→ Sleep

→ New business

→ Time management

→ Goal – are you on target?

→ Inspiration fuel.

That list can be daunting so we recommend that you start with just four dials on your dashboard. You can always add more later, but right now we want this to be a fast, at a glance, weekly update designed to inform you, not confuse you. Include PROFIT, GOAL and INSPIRATION, the fourth dial that you add is entirely up to you. Each week you will update the dash and see if the improvements you were looking for happened.

The very act of thinking about how your business is working out, and then marking those thoughts on the dashboard will make acting on them much easier. When we write something down, when we commit it to paper and know we will be back to measure our actions against the list one week later we tend to perform much better than when we just think about doing it. So yes, you could do all this in your head, it's not rocket science after all. But the act of giving it definiteness of purpose and acting on that will be the springboard that launches you and your business forward faster, and with less effort. With the dashboard created, you'll feel on top of things. Making it a regular destination to measure how you are performing against it each week will mean that you actually are on top of things.

So the first dial we asked you to add to the board is your profit. If your company is not making money, or not aligned to hit profit then this will need addressing right now. You may have savings and be able to keep going for a while, but if you are not making money and yet spending time on stuff that isn't directly related to making money then you will risk failing. Some people are not money minded and let this incredibly important dial run riot whilst they spend hours, days even choosing a new logo for the company van. It is all a complete waste of time if you are not set to make money. Profit is the lifeblood of a business. It must be your focus, and that focus be treated with great respect. So get the 'profit' dial on the dash and look at it weekly. And ensure you consider every new business purchase carefully, as it will be eating into your profit and that will effect the position of the dial. Feel proud, feel happy, feel compelled to make money. Making money may not have been your only motivator, there are probably many other reasons you wanted to make your business idea happen, but if it doesn't make money you'll inevitably have a problem. At some point, maybe when your bank account is empty, you will wish you had paid attention to your profit dial.

get the profit dial on the dash and look at it weekly

When you first thought about starting a business we asked you to consider why you wanted a business in the first place? Does that same goal or dream exist today? What does your destination look like now? It's important you keep that goal, old or new, as a focus, as a real destination that you can plot your way to. So add the 'goal' dial to your dashboard and ask, did you move closer to your goal this week? What could you do next week to move that dial in the right direction? By knowing exactly where you want to arrive at, you can focus your effort on getting there. If your raison d'être was changing the world, are you on target to do that? If it is to sell the company for 1 million, are you on track to do that, or are you just saying words and not applying the correct action to achieve it. Check that dashboard, every week on a Monday morning before you open that first email. Understand what requires your attention, appreciate how important it is not to drift off course and apply the effort required to ultimately get what you set out to get.

Now we want to talk to you about another dial that needs to be considered. It's the 'inspiration' fuel dial. This is the dial that tells you if you are feeling inspired or not. It may seem strange to consider this as such an important dial at first but think about this. You may have spent the last few years working for a company. You have spent a lot of time serving someone else's mentality and probably got quite good at it. The unsaid rules of your old office life measured people by such things as how long they spend in the office, skipping lunch, going home late and arriving for work early. Efficiency and effectiveness are words that have been banded around post-recession and staff have become good at being accountable for every hour they spend at work. Now you have your own business, are you still behaving like you work for The Man? Are you still feeling obliged to arrive early, skip lunch and go home late. Do you still feel guilty when you think of investing in yourself, your own development? Stop! Investing in your journey is integral to your company development. And that means occasionally rewarding yourself with a healthy dollop of inspiration.

Kevin Roberts, CEO Worldwide at Saatchi & Saatchi, told us '*inspiration out is a big result of inspiration in*'; and you need to take inspiration from what's outside in the real world, not from emails and search engines. So whatever business you are in you will find conferences and events going on in your field. You're the boss, if the financial dial permits it, then you can travel to an event every month. Meet other people facing similar challenges to you. Get inspired, or re-inspired if you like, go back to that place where you felt energised and ready to change the world. And that may not be a

the inspiration fuel dial tells you if you are feeling inspired or not

conference, it might be an 'away-day' to another city or
a train ride someplace. Ian has worked for himself for
11 years; he takes at least two 'inspiration jaunts' a year
where he goes to another city, reflects on his business
and refills his inspiration tank. It's part of his dashboard
management. So do not imprison yourself in a false
belief that as the business owner you can't afford to
invest in the most important asset you own, you. If a
visit to an art gallery will help your development as an
interior designer then schedule it in. It may give you just
the perspective you were looking for to apply to your
next client. What it will certainly do is provide you with
inspiration, it will get you out of the office and connected
to the real world and fuel you up. If a conference for
broadcasters will inspire you as a videographer, then
attend. You will learn about new equipment coming to
market, you can blog about it showing yourself as a
thought leader and you will get to meet other people on
a similar journey who will be willing to share valuable
intelligence. But most of all you will have a full inspiration
tank again, recharged, ready for the next part of the
journey. Every month, schedule in your fuel stop, enjoy it
and use it to network and promote your business.

The dashboard is there to help you check you are
getting what you really want and to help you focus and
fix the stuff that isn't right. So take action, the stuff that
is hitting 6 or below on the dashboard, fix it!

You're going to need to get very familiar with the
dashboard, it'll be there throughout your business
journey. Life in the Zoom cockpit will sometimes travel
at 100 mph, so it's essential to monitor and check
progress as you go. Sometimes the dials will change,
some indicators become more important as you
grow. Factors like health and spending time with the
family might become more important as you get older,
whereas at the start, chances are you'll be putting your
foot on the gas to drive up the needle.

ZOOM THINKING

1 Work out what your dashboard looks like, what dial is missing? What is the indicator specific to you that needs to be on there?

2 Take immediate action on any dials showing 6 or below.

3 Remember to include your emotional and happiness indicators as well as profit. Are you profiting emotionally as well as financially?

And that's a wrap

So there you go.

You now know the importance of business doing over business planning, how you need to think like a kid to and the importance of keeping your proposition simple. You know that ideas do not have to be perfect to launch; you can launch whilst in beta and benefit from acting on feedback from real users. You know that success is about an optimistic mindset; you also know it's inevitable you'll meet some hurdles on your way. But you understand the power of visualisation and you have the Magic Umbrella to keep you dry when the rain is pelting down on you. You will not feel daunted now when faced with the challenge of a big project; you know by taking it slice by slice and employing our 60-second decision making and 60-minute doing, that literally anything is possible.

So you know that you can do it. There are no excuses. You can take your idea, and you can make it happen. And you can make it happen rapidly.

So it's time to apply some Zoom to your idea. Good luck and tell us about your journey, we'd love to hear your story.

Thank you for reading our book

Ian and David, May 2011

thezoomguys.com

#zoombook

Zoom thinking: a checklist for action/launching your business in 60 days

1 Creating your eureka moment

1 Have you addressed the problem your product or business is trying to solve?

2 Why will your customers love it?

3 Are you in love with the idea?

2 The trouble with too much planning

1 Promise yourself you will not spend time trying to guess the future.

2 Thinking back to Pascal's story, what is the 'Why' for your business?

3 What is the 'How' for your business?

3 Getting to grips with your mission

1 Promise yourself you will not get involved in a business that is not a natural fit.

2 Are you in the right mindset to start your business?

3 What are you prepared to sacrifice to succeed?

4 Set a goal

1 Focus on your goal, and work backwards.

2 Identify your timeline for how to achieve your goal in 60 days.

3 Don't try and do everything at once. Make sure your goals are manageable.

5 A licence to be curious

1 Start a scrapbook to capture your research.

2 Get out of the house! Talk to people and listen.

3 See how other people are doing things well; be alert to how that can influence your own business.

6 Shaping your idea

1 What is the most important benefit your business offers?

2 Describe your business in 140 characters or less.

3 How are you going to make your idea boxable?

7 Imagine it

1 Start making visualisation part of your business thinking.

2 Visualise your goal. Get very familiar with how it looks and feels.

3 Think how the Miracle Question can help you understand what your customers want.

8 Think like a speedboat

1 Agility wins, so be ready for rapid change.

2 Re-tune your business thinking to embrace serendipity.

3 Remember, you're a speedboat now, so there's no room for baggage. So don't bring it onboard.

9 Embrace business doing

1 Rethink your schedule tomorrow. How can you shift focus so you're spending as much time as possible Doing?

2 What Doing-Tools can you introduce to fast track your business?

3 Are you making a big dent in your to-do list?

10 Salami steps

1 Go and buy a pack of Post-its and a marker pen. Clear your kitchen table and start mapping out your journey.

2 Sixty minutes to get this done. You'll be amazed at how much can be achieved.

3 Sixty seconds to make a decision. No excuses!

11 Telling your story

1 Your story will differentiate you from the competition and make you memorable in the minds of your customers. So, craft a convincing but authentic story, based on personal experience and emotion rather than on dry facts and stats.

2 People love passion, so tell your story like you care about it passionately.

3 What's our story? Find out here: **www.thezoomguys.com**

12 Think like a kid

1 How can you apply thinking like a kid to your business?

2 Is your website just too complicated and your offering needing communicating in straightforward language?

3 Are you trying to add too many features or buttons to something that works perfectly well?

13 The power of collaboration

1 Get used to looking for opportunities to collaborate with other people.

2 Be willing to help others, because you never know where that might lead.

3 What kind of space or cluster might help your business? Do you need to hang out in a co-working space, join a networking club?

14 Magic Umbrella

1 When trouble strikes, put that umbrella up.

2 Now the umbrella is up, you can park your problem.

3 Go for that run around the block and start making serotonin.

4 Get calm, get focused on solutions.

15 Launch in beta

1 Feel the pressure of going live.

2 Launch as fast as you can, better to have a near-perfect idea launch than you never launch your perfect idea.

3 Use social media to listen to customers – get feedback, monitor, evaluate and tweak accordingly.

16 Your Launch Day

1 Celebrate. Mark the moment with whatever currency of celebration is appropriate. Pop open the champagne; order the Nando's chicken, whatever.

2 Press 'Pause'. Stand back, reflect, pat yourself on the back, see how that moment matched your expectations, your goals, your visualisations.

3 Refuel your inspiration tank. Take a night away in a hotel, a run in the park, an afternoon at an art gallery – whatever it takes – to get inspired and to have the energy to deal with whatever is next.

17 Create a dashboard

1 Work out what your dashboard looks like, what dial is missing? What is the indicator specific to you that needs to be on there?

2 Take immediate action on any dials showing 6 or below.

3 Remember to include your emotional and happiness indicators as well as profit. Are you profiting emotionally as well as financially?

Index

This book was made with the help of:

32 train journeys
203 espressos
4 Moleskine notebooks
96 Post It notes